The Gospel in a Strange, New World

Westminster Studies in Christian Communication

Kendig Brubaker Cully, General Editor

The Gospel in a Strange, New World

THEODORE O. WEDEL

THE WESTMINSTER PRESS
Philadelphia

LIBRARY OF CONGRESS CATALOG CARD No. 63-8161

PRINTED IN THE UNITED STATES OF AMERICA

To

THE DEAN
THE FACULTY
and
THE STUDENTS
of the
Episcopal Theological School
in Cambridge, Massachusetts

who welcomed me as a member of their community during the year when the Kellogg Lectures were delivered

1961 to 1962

Contents

A Note on Westminster Studies
in Christian Communication

These Studies are predicated on the ground that the Christian faith needs to be made relevant to persons in the modern world in terms of the dynamic nature of the faith itself and the channels that are capable of conveying such a faith. In itself any technique of communication conceivably could serve as well for secular as for religious ends. In this series a wide variety of means and methods of communication will be analyzed in the light of their availability to, and suitability for, the particular tasks that the Christian church faces in bringing the realities of faith to bear upon the life of actual persons in the contemporary situation.

Oftentimes in the past, techniques have been viewed almost as ends in themselves. Or, they have been taken over uncritically from the secular culture without being subjected to adequate scrutiny as to whether they are appropriate for the church's use. On the other hand, sometimes the church has been blind to the life situations of the present to such an extent as to ignore the real ways in which people's lives are influenced by all that impinges on them. In the latter case, the church has failed to bring the life-giving power of the gospel to bear on contemporary culture because of a lack of understanding of, or appreciation for, the means of communication that have been proved capable of changing lives and societies.

Involving as it does both the "What" and the "How," the whole question of the communication of the gospel in the modern world is pivotal in the present juncture of history. The present Studies will be aimed at bringing the "What" and the "How" together fruitfully. These books are designed to make a contribution to the ongoing conversations across boundaries. Theology, Biblical studies, sociology, cultural anthropology, psychology, education, art, letters, science, and the other disciplines all have something to say to one another. In our present concern, " communication " refers to the way in which the Christian faith can come into conjunction with what is happening in the total world of life and ideas in the middle decades of the twentieth century. In each of these Studies attention will focus on some important aspect of the basic question: How can the church most effectively preach, teach, and otherwise manifest the gospel in the growing edges of man's present-day culture? No aspect of man's actual situation is alien to such a question. No medium of communication should fail to come under scrutiny if, as Christians, we are eager to have the Word of God confront a confused generation powerfully and compellingly.

Each volume in Westminster Studies in Christian Communication will be an authentic voice of one perceptive interpreter. No effort has been made to suggest to any writer what " line " he ought to follow. Each work will be adjudged by the readers on its own merits. The writers themselves conceivably might disagree heartily with regard to certain presuppositions or conclusions held by their colleagues. All this will be to the good if the result of these Studies should be the stimulating of many conversations. Yet all the writers have in mind a focus that is realistic, an emphasis that is practical, and a discussion that is timely. The only request made of the authors is that they speak out of their knowledge to the very heart and mind of our times. Depth without dullness, breadth without diffuseness, challenge without sentimentality — these, at least, it is hoped, will be characteristics of all the Studies. We are grateful to those who have consented to share in this venture into communication, and we commend their work as in itself an integral part of the church's task of communication.

KENDIG BRUBAKER CULLY
General Editor

Evanston, Illinois

Preface

In February, 1962, the Episcopal Theological School in Cambridge, Massachusetts, accorded me the privilege of delivering these lectures before an audience of alumni of the school and such students as could spare time from their studies for one of those extra calls to audience participation that burden a seminary's calendar. An annual lectureship in memory of his father, Frederic Rogers Kellogg, had been established in 1953 by the Reverend Frederic Brainerd Kellogg. The school, accordingly, welcomes each year a scholar or missionary or, as in the present instance, a teacher temporarily a member of the faculty, to share with the seminary community his insights into the gospel and the church's mission in our bewildered time. The honor accorded me of joining this roster of lecturers is one that deserves far more expressions of gratitude than can be embodied in a preface. I have tried to say something in one of the lectures in behalf of the ministry of listening as a symbol of Christian grace. I even recall a chance remark in one of Emil Brunner's writings defining a Christian as a man who can listen. Listening, by its very nature, involves a sacrifice of time and attention, both of which are precious personal possessions not lightly surrendered. The usual etiquette of parting words at the close of a lecture — the listeners thanking the speaker — ought, by rights, to be reversed. The audience has been the prime bestower of a gift. For this gift, as I look back on my recent platform privilege, I give heartfelt thanks.

The lectures, now appearing in book form and thus called "chapters," have been here and there expanded and are guilty of some repetitions, especially as an introductory essay enlarges on a topic touched on in Chapter I. The reader's sympathetic understanding of such hazards of authorship is solicited.

T. O. W.

Introduction

A future historian of theological trends in the twentieth century may be surprised to find how suddenly books and pamphlets embodying the word "communication" in their titles emerged on publishers' lists in the decades of the 1950's and 1960's. They do not thus appear in bibliographical listings in the preceding decades. I can give personal testimony to this somewhat strange publication phenomenon. I had been asked to conduct a seminar on Christian communication in the fall of 1954 at the Ecumenical Institute of the World Council of Churches in Geneva. The reason for my being chosen for this pedagogic venture could be traced to the fact that for some fifteen years I had been on the staff of the College of Preachers in Washington, D.C., an institution whose very name implies dedication to the ministry of communication — even if only by way of sermons. In trying to prepare for my instructional task, I explored bibliographical resources. Books on secular mass communication media existed in abundance, but I met a virtual blank in my search for theologically oriented literature on the subject — at least when the word "communication" had been honored on a title page. Not that no champions for the Christian faith had as yet put pen to paper, of course. If the search turned to books on library shelves under the topics of evangelism and missions, a whole array of volumes beckoned. The comparatively sudden appearance of theological literature employing prominently the word "communication" may, accord-

ingly, be of interest mainly to students of semantics. Yet, I suspect, more is involved in the bibliographical story than merely
this verbal innovation.

" These are great days for theology," so reads the lyric close
of a recent book on the New Testament. " The queen of the
sciences is once again coming into her own. Men are beginning
to see that a Christianity without a theology is not Christianity
at all." The author continues with a description of the rich
variety of theological revivals which mark our age. A common
denominator, however, exists. " All are realizing anew the importance of Biblical theology." [1]

No one at all acquainted with the schools of theology of
our time — at least those enjoying full academic freedom — can
fail to echo this shout of rejoicing. But an observer of the
shape of religion on the American scene beyond the borders
of theological classrooms finds his rejoicing brought to a sudden halt. The contemporary theological renaissance is as yet
largely monopolized by an academic elite. We are undoubtedly
witnessing in the present generation a " revival of religion "
in the land, though the ambiguity of the concept " religion "
(I have something to say on this topic in my opening chapter)
burdens at once our statistical optimism. Testimony is ready to
hand, for example, that the present popularity of religion is
being manifested primarily, on the part of the laity at least, in
the activism of the typical suburban parish house, with its
allurements of organizational " togetherness." Such activism
can flourish alongside of what must be realistically labeled
theological illiteracy. The younger clergy of the churches,
beneficiaries as they are of the theological renaissance in the
seminaries of the land, are becoming aware of the fact that, if
they cannot in good conscience surrender their vocation as
ministers of the Word in favor of what an observer, cited in
one of my later chapters, describes colloquially as spiritual
" baby-sitting," they confront a communication problem of gigantic proportions.

The most obvious symptom of the theological illiteracy of

the laity in the churches is their ignorance of the Bible. Since I have devoted only a few paragraphs of my opening chapter to the problem which this ignorance presents to the church's teaching ministry, I venture to honor it with some expanded discussion in this Introduction.

Visitors from the younger churches of Asia and Africa often speak of our American Christianity as a "Bible-starved Christianity." The indictment is surely deserved. This vacuum of ignorance may not have been recognized as serious in the generation before the arrival of our theological renaissance when we were to a large extent satisfied with a humanist version of the gospel for which a minimal Biblical anchorage seemed to suffice. If the Christian faith could be defined as little more than commitment to perfectionist moral ideals, even though the teachings and example of Jesus were glorified as necessary validations, the Old Testament accorded honor only as anachronistic background and the letters of Paul only as now equally dated footnotes, Biblical illiteracy presented no very serious problem. A generation at least, its older members still with us, grew up under the reign of this Bible-starved Christianity, and the ignorance of the fathers is being visited upon their children.

I shall not burden this introductory essay with the story of the debacle of this reductionist Christianity. As the New Testament scholar cited earlier attests, our generation is beginning to see that a Christianity of mere ethical ideals "without a theology is not Christianity at all." In the seminaries of the churches such a "Christianity without theology" has long been outgrown; indeed, many young seminary graduates are scarcely aware that it once reigned supreme in pulpit and church school and still has deep roots in popular understanding of the Christian faith. One reason, accordingly, for the emergence of "communication" as a crucial concern of the church in our era of theological revival is the discovery on the part of the church's teaching ministry that it confronts a vacuum of illiteracy, unsuspected earlier, which demands the dedication to a ministry of communication of the best the church has by way of imaginative pedagogic gifts.

Our Bible-starved Christianity is in danger of suffering the dread fate of amnesia. We no longer know what we are. For to be a Christian at all is to be a member of a faith community, a community unified by loyalty to a God who has revealed himself in history. The Bible is the record of that revelation, a drama of the " mighty acts " of the God in whom the faith community places its trust and loyalty. The historic creeds of Christianity are scenario recitals of this drama — the story in miniature — from a time " before all worlds " to the establishment of a Kingdom that " shall have no end."

Can a man be a Christian unless he knows this drama and knows, further, that he is himself still one of its dramatis personae? Every people or communal group lives by a story of some kind, one with a past, a present, and a future. The lure of communism, to cite an example, consists in its invitation to prospective converts to become actors in a drama which, like the Christian story, has a past and a future, its still awaited last act a promised utopian heaven on earth. And this is only one analogy out of many that could be culled from the history of the cultures and religions of mankind. The necessity of having a story to give meaning to existence can be seen in our personal lives also. A man who has lost the memory of his past and suffers amnesia has lost his identity. " The complete loss of one's identity," says a wise Roman Catholic theologian, " is, with all propriety of theological definition, hell. In diminished form it is insanity." [2] Can we imagine what would happen to our national life if, as the American people, we should corporately suffer amnesia, our history a memory blank? We too would have lost our identity as a people, our clue to what being an American means. Yet an analogous fate threatens, as already suggested, the illiterate Christianity of suburbia unless it recovers its identity by way of memory of its historical past. And that involves a return to the Bible.

That communication of the thought world of the Bible presents difficulties in our time is, alas, fairly obvious. Indeed, the problem is occupying the attention of the most gifted of the theological minds of our day. Those familiar with the writings of the contemporary doctors of the schools — the names of Karl Barth, Rudolf Bultmann, Paul Tillich, and a score more come readily to remembrance — need scarcely to be reminded that here is an area of much theological dialogue today. The strange, conceptual world of the Bible, so we are told, must be reinterpreted so as to become intelligible once more to an age of scientific enlightenment. That older world clothed its religious truths in mythological language against a background of a three-story universe. It spoke familiarly of theophanies in the clouds of our earthly sky, of miracles, of angelic and demonic powers. The communicating task assigned to our time is to demythologize or at least to reinterpret this now strange Biblical imagery. And to a large extent the masters of Biblical scholarship are surely right. The future of the communicating ministry of the church as it confronts the march of cultural change in days to come may depend on the success of their efforts. Gratitude should be the church's response.

Those of us, however, who belong to the humbler ranks in the hierarchy of the church's communicators, such as the parish minister and the church school teacher, are not to be blamed for being frequently a puzzled lot. Nor shall I presume in this brief introductory essay to write a manual for our baffling pedagogic task. We shall have the dialogue of the church's theologians with us for a long time and we must listen to it. But the ongoing vocation of communicating the gospel in parish pulpit and church school classroom cannot wait until the learned doctors have resolved all the problems of interpreting the Bible. The Bible, with its symbolic language not demythologized, is still read Sunday by Sunday in our churches. The hymns we sing still speak familiarly of angels, of seraphim and cherubim, and echo verse upon verse of an unexpurgated Old and New Testament. And we shall have this Bible and these hymnbooks with us for a long time also — a simple fact that seminary professors at times forget. The instruction of children in the church school is in the hands of lay folk for whom the language of theological classrooms is far more strange than the language of Genesis or of the Gospel of Mark or even of the letters of Paul. And thus it has been from the church's earliest days, and will be for any foreseeable future, above all, in the little mission flocks in educationally under-privileged lands. Paul's words, as he addressed his flock of simple Christians in Corinth, can surely apply to us also: "Consider your call, brethren; not many of you were wise according to worldly standards, not many were powerful, not many were of noble birth" (I Cor. 1:26).

I venture to suggest, therefore, that those of us charged with this ongoing ministry of Christian communication take courage. For, clearly, the first step in communicating the Christian story does not require expert theological learning. Let the story interpret itself. Helpful guides for simple Bible reading are available in abundance. Familiarity with the Biblical text itself, though puzzling passages may have been left for later attention and some even ignored (the book of Leviticus, perhaps), will at least have filled the vacuum of ignorance which blocks any second step. The first acquaintance with a play by Shakespeare like *Hamlet* had best be the play itself without learned footnotes. We let the sweep of the story have its say — its plot and design. Questions will come, but they can wait. The Bible, too, has a plot and a design. Without familiarity with this, the details (we usually hear the Bible read in public worship only in snippets) frequently make little sense.

The experience of many a preacher and teacher in the ongoing life of the churches parallels, I am convinced, my own in discovering that many a layman who, with even only a little help, is reintroduced to the Bible, sophisticated and modern though he be, can take "myth, miracle, and legend" in his stride. The theological climate of our era has brought a great boon of which the church's laity can be grateful beneficiaries. Communication of the Christian faith was once thought to consist in the presentation of a doctrinal system, weighted with propositions and truths, each buttressed by a Biblical proof text, and thus a body of divine pronouncements. But this Biblical literalism is now happily superseded by the insight that the primary revelation given us in the Bible is not in the form of a dogmatic system, but in act and deed. The theology of the Bible is recital theology — the record of historical events in which the people who experienced the events discerned God's self-revelation as Creator, Judge, and Redeemer. The recording, however, remains human recording. Communal memory, in a prescientific age, might be expected to weave into its recollections of the past legendary material as well as eye-witness reports. Are we not familiar in the memories we preserve of the past history of our own families with tales and stories which have received embroidery in much retelling so as to partake of the mysterious and the miraculous?

Given the clue to the Bible as, from the human side, a people's history book, even the concept of myth need no longer shock the modern reader. The story of Adam and Eve in a garden is by now a familiar example. Could there be a better picturing of the dialogue with God experienced still today by every man and woman? We all still meet God walking in the cool of the day and hear the call, " Where are you? " That this portrayal takes the form of a myth or saga, a story imaginatively projected into the past, does not rob it of its profound meaning. Similarly, it should not cause surprise that the Biblical writers picture a last act in the divine revelation drama — a future Last Judgment — in colorful imagery also. Indeed, an educational ministry that trusts the Bible's own way of communicating its message, even if this means that we must make our peace with mythological imagery, can receive much encouragement from contemporary Biblical scholarship itself. One trusted Biblical scholar, to cite an example, has this to say:

The presentation of abstract dogma cannot be the primary teaching method of the church. In part this is because propositional dogmatics lacks the color, the flexibility, the movement of the Bible, and because it attempts to freeze into definite, prosaic, rationality that which was never intended by the Bible so to be frozen and which by its very nature cannot be so construed. . . .

In order to present the proclamation of the Lord of history we can only use the Biblical myths; there is no other way of communicating Biblical truth.[3]

Communication of the Christian faith cannot, of course, end with a cure of Biblical illiteracy. The revelation drama of the Bible is not museum history. We are still actors in its uncompleted action. We are still on the stage. The theological pioneers of our era are right in demanding that Biblical symbols must be reinterpreted as living answers to living questions. When they tell us, for example, that these Biblical symbols must become existential (that sometimes puzzling word), this is what they mean. The climactic act in the Biblical epic is a coming down of a Son of God into our human life and a dying on a cross and a resurrection. Communication of the Christian faith will not be complete unless there is a death and a resurrection in our lives also.

At this point, however, this introductory essay will pause. Lifting the burden of religious illiteracy from the church's ministry of communication is only a first step. This is the church's intramural task. Even if the task were perfectly accomplished, every layman a Biblical theologian, the church's vocation to communicate the gospel would have only begun. For the church would then still confront the world and the call to communicate the gospel to the world. Knowledge of the Christian story is privilege facing a demand: "Go therefore and make disciples of all nations" (Matt. 28:19). The chapters that now follow, with only a backward glance here and there to the church's intramural vocation, will try to explore what such a ministry of communication to those outside the church's protecting walls may involve.

Chapter I

The Gospel in a Strange, New World

> In the sea of life enisled,
>   With echoing straits between us thrown,
> Dotting the shoreless watery wild,
>   We mortal millions live alone.
> The islands feel the enclasping flow,
> And then their endless bounds they know.[4]

Thus Matthew Arnold, a hundred years ago, in a mood of disillusionment with modern visions of progress, called attention to a problem in human relations which even an achieved technological utopia would leave unsolved — the problem of creating community, of building bridges between islands of isolation, of alleviating the haunting human burden of loneliness.

Have the generations since Matthew Arnold's era brought us nearer to a solution of this problem? Viewed superficially, the scientific triumphs of the twentieth century do seem to have moved men out of the prisons of isolation into intimate contact with one another. We can fly the air and pay a visit to a friend living in the antipodes within days or hours. The telephone and the radio bring a voice from the most distant continent or island or even ships on the high seas into our homes with time annihilated. If the spoken word is a test of relationship, the question once asked of Jesus, "Who is my neighbor?" almost seems absurd. The techniques of communication have made solitude or the blessed anodyne of silence a rare luxury. Our age is receiving many names. One of the newest slogans on the scene defines it as an age of publicity. It is the age of sound. The marvel of progress in the arts and techniques of communication could well halt for a time, as far as a further need for media of external contact between man and man is concerned.

Yet the moment we look beneath the spectacular surface of our mass communication era, a paradox meets the eye. Join to the word " communication " the preposition " of " — yielding the phrase " communication of " — and the opportunity of spreading an item of news or appealing for a cause is almost limitless. Millions of ears may be prepared or even compelled to listen. But join to the word " communication " the preposition " between " — yielding the phrase " communication between," with its implication of a meeting of man with man — and a vacuum appears.[5] Mass communication is revealed as essentially a monologue addressed to masses of listening ears. This is not a real meeting of person with person, not *communication*. It is the opposite of what has been called the sacrament of dialogue. Each listener to the monologue listens for himself alone. Isolation and anonymity have not been conquered. Their pain may merely have received an anesthetic. The title of a recent popular book of social analysis describes the paradox of our mass communication era: we are today's members of a " lonely crowd." We are isolated atoms within an increasingly compacted mass.

Time magazine a few years ago quoted a prominent radio artist's comment on this mass communication paradox. He harked back, in a moment of reflection, to an earlier period in his career when he still harbored the illusion that he was addressing a community of listeners. " In those days," he confessed, " we were all talking to the ladies and gentlemen of the radio audience. I decided that there wasn't any such audience. There was just one guy or one girl off somewhere by themselves. Hell, if they were together, they'd have something better to do than listen to the radio." To paraphrase the radio

artist's observation, they would enjoy "communication between." [6]

I have brought to our attention thus far only one facet of
the problem of communication. Many others could receive
analysis. The problem is of importance in our common cultural
life. The specialist in science seeks converse with his fellow
scientist in an ivory tower next door. Both are isolated from
communal discourse with those outside academic walls. The
advertiser scours heaven and earth for symbols of communication designed to produce consumer capitulation. Nowhere,
however, is the importance of the problem of communication
more clearly underscored than in the life of the church. Wherever the church's task of mission and evangelism is today being
studied under a recognition of the church's minority status on
our globe or its engagement in a confrontation with a world
dedicating itself to secular idolatries, the problem of communication leaps to the forefront of attention. On the ecumenical scene few themes are more widely discussed than the
question: How to communicate the gospel?

Mass media of communication beckon. Nor are they being
ignored. Religious radio and television programs are at the tip
of a dial-tuning finger. If all that were required to convert an
indifferent world were a voice before a microphone and an
electronic multiplication device, our age could be Christian
overnight. The number of listeners to Sunday sermons in the
churches spread round our globe is itself still astoundingly
large. If each hearer of the word were to go forth as a bearer
of the full power of the gospel, our era in history might see
again what Christianity's earliest centuries witnessed — a world
turned upside down. Clearly, the problem of communicating
the gospel becomes real on a deeper level than that of means
of verbal publicity.

How to communicate the gospel? We are victims of naïve
illusions if we think there is an easy answer. The Apostles'
Creed, one of our most familiar summaries of the Christian
faith, can be recited in forty seconds. No dictionary is needed

by the average listener to apprehend its verbal meaning. Yet
it would be folly to trust it to win converts by itself. On occasion we may register surprise as we read The Acts of the
Apostles to note how promptly the earliest sermons produced a
harvest of believers. Though probably a bit longer than our
miniature pulpit homilies, they surely were not encyclopedic
presentations of Christian doctrine. But the age in which they
were preached had an advantage over our own. It was prepared for the good news by centuries of religious disciplines.
We of the twentieth century could envy those early witnesses.
Theirs was the world of "the fullness of time." Even a proclamation addressed to the Gentiles could take for granted an
understanding of most of the language of the New Testament.
No one had to explain the meaning of an altar, or of atoning
sacrifice, or of the symbols of an eschatological backdrop to
human existence. For a Roman citizen, to cite one example,
Vergil's *Aeneid,* especially its awesome picturization of judgment after death in the matchless Sixth Book, could be a preparation for the gospel. Many a preacher today in secularized
suburbia might envy Paul as he preached to the Greek intelli-
gentsia on Mars' Hill. An unknown god was, after all, still
acknowledged as a god. I am reminded of a preacher, wise for
our era, who paraphrased the first of the Ten Commandments
to read: "Thou shalt have at least one god."

In a word, we are today trying to communicate the gospel,
both inside and outside the borders of what once was Christendom, to a world in which the very language of the Bible —
the "language of Canaan," as it has been called — has become
increasingly strange, if not unknown. To cite again a concrete
example, which may have to carry the burden of a longer argument, the contemporary poet W. H. Auden recently called
attention to the fact that a Biblical symbol for Christ like
"Lamb of God," in a culture mainly urban, "is likely to evoke
ridiculous images." In its Latin version, *Agnus Dei,* it "has
the attraction at least of a magical and musical spell." [7] The
whole mythological imagery of the Bible, at home in a three-

story universe, so Rudolf Bultmann somewhat violently reminds us, has vanished into a forgotten world of thought. We
must demythologize, or, as less radical critics might say, at
least remythologize or reinterpret many a Biblical symbol.

An article in *The Ecumenical Review* by a leader in the Department on the Laity of the World Council of Churches describes vividly this loss of meaning which even some of the
most familiar words of Biblical speech have suffered in our
time. The author has the European scene in mind, but his diagnosis of a major problem in communication is worth our attention on this side of the Atlantic also.

A word like conversion, for example, has no longer about it any of
the radiant luster of the deliverance that is experienced when a man
turns to Christ. Instead, it is associated if not with the idea of painful self-exposures in which immoral things are brought to light, then
with the excesses of mainly professional evangelists. Repentance
seems far removed from the Messianic anticipatory joy that the
purifying immersion of John the Baptist signified. We think of the
fines or of the penalties imposed by a policeman or a teacher. Grace,
too, has lost all meaning for many people. They know that grace is
something good. The Word has not yet lost its illuminating power
completely. There is a light shining over it as there was over the
stable at Bethlehem. But men do not find the way there through
that sign. It is no longer grasped that grace means the wiping out
of our offenses by God with a generosity compared to which the
pardoning of a murderer before his judge is nothing, that it oper-
ates in all of us through Jesus Christ. Faith is historical belief in the
facts of salvation and the message of the Bible. Thus the Word has
not yet completely lost its meaning. Through experience in human
relationships, do you believe in me? I have faith in you. There remains at least a trace of the original sense of it. Sin has entirely
ceased to be associated with God and is seen only in relation to a
morally understood church or pastorate that seeks to take away from
people the little pleasures they have. The prototype of the sinner is
the man or woman who lives more or less frivolously. The fact that
sin as a dangerous separation from God is found in its diabolical
self-awareness among morally blameless men and women is never
dreamed of.[8]

Clearly, we are at only the beginning of solving a problem in communication of gigantic proportions.

We meet, on the American scene at least, a further embarrassment. Ignorance of the authentic Christian faith can exist alongside, or in the very midst of, a flourishing religious institutionalism. Books are multiplying which attempt to diagnose this paradox. The word "religion" has so long gathered about itself an aura of sanctity that a shock awaits many a reader when he is told that "religion" is not necessarily a good thing at all, that it can become a most dangerous barrier to a true relationship with the God of the Bible. This will be a hard lesson for us to absorb on our side of the Atlantic, although a little review of Old Testament prophecy could lessen the shock. The experience of our Christian brethren in Europe may come to our aid, since theirs is, in some sense, approaching the opposite of our condition — a secularism *without* religion. More than one European visitor, far from envying us as we enjoy the popularity of our religious activism — our palatial parish houses and our organizational whirl of "togetherness" — voices warnings of dangers ahead. Karl Barth can write an unforgettable essay on "Religion as Unbelief." [9] Dr. Visser 't Hooft, General Secretary of the World Council of Churches, entitles an eloquent chapter "God or Religion." [10] Theologically alert observers in our own midst are no less vocal. We are growing familiar with descriptions of our reduction of the Christianity of the cross to mere "religion in general," [11] of our yielding to an idolatry of an amiable syncretism, the worship of a god genial and jolly, manageable, comfortable, and easily accepted as sanction for our American way of life. Will Herberg can cite with approval the outburst of a fundamentalist preacher: "I will tell you, brethren, God *hates* religion; he wants faith." [12] Archbishop Temple's now famous saying, "God is not especially interested in religion," has startled many a sermon listener. Reinhold Niebuhr, indeed, puts the issue bluntly: "Religion qua religion is naturally idolatrous, accentuating rather than diminishing the self-worship of men and nations by assuring them an ultimate sanction for their dearest desires." [13]

The layman unfamiliar with theological subtleties cannot be blamed if he meets such attacks on a sacred word with incomprehension. Yet he, too, can be led to see the ambiguity and even danger of "religion in general" by seeing that ambiguity and danger concretely exhibited in his life of prayer. The word "prayer," like the word "religion," is surrounded by a halo. It takes but a few moments' thought, however, to realize that prayer was not invented by Christians. Prayer has existed from the dawn of time. It has been addressed to monstrous idols. Jesus, in the Gospel narrative, was subjected to the temptation to address prayer to Satan himself in place of God. Demonic "principalities and powers" are all about us enticing to worship and prepared to grant the petitioner's requests. "Religion as unbelief" is no empty phrase. When we expose ourselves to a dialogue with the God of the Biblical revelation, nothing receives more penetrating judgment than precisely our life of prayer. "Let thy merciful ears, O Lord, be open to the prayers of thy humble servants," so reads one of the church's ancient collects, "and, that they may obtain their petitions, make them to ask such things as shall please thee." To ask such things as shall please the holy God — is that easy? "You do not have, because you do not ask," says The Letter of James (ch. 4:2). The Lord's Prayer, seen in this light, becomes a foretaste of Judgment Day. How many of our self-regarding petitions can stand that test — our *askings* under judgment! In prayer we enter God's confessional, where our masks are torn off and where "all hearts are open, all desires known."

Is it difficult, indeed, to find examples of petitions in our own prayer life which voice desires that the holy God must see as an offense? Few disciplines in piety are more wholesome for us than a realistic transcript of many a petition that we arrogantly present before our Creator and Judge. A recent delightfully written volume, *He Sent Leanness*, can bring a blush of shame to many readers. Here, for example, is a version of the familiar General Confession, reworded so as to express the actual prayer life of the "natural man."

Benevolent and easygoing Father: We have occasionally been guilty of errors of judgment. We have lived under the deprivations of heredity and the disadvantages of environment. We have sometimes failed to act in accordance with common sense. We have done the best we could in the circumstances; and have been careful not to ignore the common standards of decency; and we are glad to think that we are fairly normal. Do thou, O Lord, deal lightly with our infrequent lapses. Be thine own sweet self with those who admit they are not perfect; according to the unlimited tolerance which we have a right to expect from thee. And grant as an indulgent Parent that we may hereafter continue to live a harmless and happy life and keep our self-respect.[14]

Clearly, it is precisely our religious life which is the battleground of faith. Idolatry tempts us on every side, and idolatry can be very religious. The priests of Baal in the story of Elijah's battle in behalf of Israel's God were not lacking in religious zeal. "Cry aloud, for he is a god," Elijah mocked his rivals; "either he is musing, or he has gone aside, or he is on a journey, or perhaps he is asleep and must be awakened." (I Kings 18:27.) Baal worship was serious business. The confrontation of Christianity today with non-Christian religions is again with worship traditions many of which, judged by the test of sacrificial devotion, can put most of us Christians to shame.

It should be said, of course, that the word "religion" will not be banished from our vocabulary by such prophetic outbursts. Christianity simply *is* one of the world's religions and cannot escape its historic vocation. It cannot live without a religious cult and religious institutional forms. But many an uncomfortable word of an Amos or Jeremiah and of the Jesus of the Gospel story himself can remind us that it is our "religion" which will be exposed to relentless scrutiny when the God of all lesser gods and Lord of all lesser lords confronts us at his ultimate assize. What or whom have we really worshiped? Shall we possibly be numbered among those whom the New Testament writer describes as "holding the *form* of religion but denying the power of it" (II Tim. 3:5, italics mine)?

Must we not in all honesty confess that much of our religion in America is at best a thin coating over a secularism that lives a life of its own far removed from sanctuary or parish hall? City and suburb, factory, and such remnants of family pietism as are still left us, exist in separate compartments of interest and concern. An unbridged chasm divides church and world.

To realize what this means, especially as the church confronts its evangelizing mission in our time, we can listen with profit to our European brethren. On the other side of the Atlantic, as already hinted, the issue of church and world, or God and secular man, has assumed clearer outline. A remnant hold of Christianity on the citizenry of western European nations is, of course, still in existence. Indeed, many an American visitor is astounded to find that while church attendance among the working class at least is at a minimum, children are still christened, marriages are still church ceremonies, and the church still buries the dead. A sizable middle-class loyalty to church attendance has not vanished either. Hence the difference between Europe and America may be less than a first observation might suggest. Our social structure has merely widened the embrace of this middle class. In both environments the schism between church and world has become an acute problem. It is seen as a problem even when, as in churches anchored in the Roman Catholic tradition, a cult orthodoxy protects the sanctuary and the pulpit from mere "religion in general."

It is surely significant that nowhere is the necessity of a new approach by the church to the world more boldly explored than in Roman Catholicism itself. An analysis of the present danger of a church's finding itself isolated from the world in a ghetto (Europeans still use the phrase "bourgeois ghetto") is voiced by many Roman Catholic observers. One of the best known of such confessions is Abbé Michonneau's *Revolution in a City Parish.* Though the scene is set in France, in what has received the descriptive title "France Pagan," its realistic appraisal of the church's evangelizing task in our time is applicable to virtually the entire remnant of Christendom in the West.

What is the worth, as Christians, of this crowd that we see in church? Do they love one another? Are they a unified element of the community? Did they come to fulfill an obligation for their own salvation, or did they come to strengthen and feed a life which they want to spread? What kind of example are they going to be to the great mass of indifferent souls among whom they live? Will they be pretty much like everyone else around them, except for a weekly habit peculiar to them? When others look at this band of the faithful, will they have a mind to become Christians? Is it not more often just the opposite—"If that is being Christian! No thanks. Not for me!" [15]

The tension between church and world is certainly not new. Solutions have varied from virtually total severance and withdrawal of the church from the world to a dominance of the church over culture such as the medieval centuries partially witnessed.[16] What remained common in all these varieties of adjustments, however, was the retention throughout of at least some sense of the church's missionary vocation. Even the monastic ideal was still subsumed under this mission call. This call is at the heart of some of the startling new incarnations of "monasticism" in both Roman Catholicism and Protestantism in our time. The papal encyclical *Provida Mater* (1948) makes provision for "secular institutes." Laymen and laywomen take vows, usually temporary, to observe the three classical counsels of poverty, chastity, and obedience, but remain fully involved in the temporal affairs of the secular order. The Taizé Community of Protestant France, as well as the German evangelical academies and other "new life centers" in both Europe and America, which invite to temporary withdrawal from the world, present further illustrations of how the monastic ideal can itself be transformed into an instrument for secular evangelism.[17]

In most Protestant history, during which the monastic ideal was repudiated (revived in Anglicanism only within the last hundred years), the call to the church to witness *against* the world found one of its responses in the Pietistic movements and sects. These can boast of having been the seedbed of the foreign missionary outreach of the Protestant churches of the past two centuries. But the motive for this evangelical missionary activity was, all too frequently, the rescue of individuals from the world, not confronting the world itself with the gospel or training the convert to witness to and in that world. The latter was as if left to the devil alone. One writer has interpreted this motive as if it based itself on a revised version of John 3:16: " God so feared the world that he gave the church in order that some might be saved out of the world." [18] This is admittedly exaggerated satire; nor does a recalling of the original Johannine text solve offhand the church-world problem. Nevertheless, our era is witnessing a radical reexamination by evangelical theologians of Pietism's apparent limitation placed upon God's rule over his world. Pietism is being boldly criticized for its blindness to the fact that the Bible asserts God's rule and the Lordship of Christ over the world as well as the church. " Creation and redemption," so one theologian gives expression to a repentant Pietism, " were brought into opposition with each other. The first and second articles (of the Apostles' Creed) were torn asunder. The world was voided of God's presence." [19]

We should be on our guard, to be sure, when we dismiss too easily the Pietist's conviction that loyalty to Christ involves withdrawal from the world. Some break between world and church is sheer necessity to preserve the people of God from surrendering their vocation as a " colony of heaven " (Phil. 3:20, Moffatt's translation) called to live by standards of conduct under the rule of God and not of worldly conformity.

Paul's command to the church of Corinth is one of many in the New Testament that warn against the loss of the church's identity in an alluring pagan environment. "Therefore," says the apostle, "come out from them, and be separate from them, says the Lord." (II Cor. 6:17.) If we turn to a concordance of the Bible and run our eyes over verse after verse in which the "world" is the theme, we confront a paradox of no easy solution. "My kingship is not of this world" is a saying of our Lord himself (John 18:36). "Do not be conformed to this world" is a further warning voiced by Paul (Rom. 12:2), and the verse has many analogues. In a later chapter this paradox of the church as distinct from the world and yet in the world with a message of God's love for the world will have to receive further attention.

Whatever may be the final solution of the paradox a preliminary warning is, however, clearly justified. Something has gone wrong whenever the call to withdrawal and separateness is interpreted as justifying a ghetto existence behind safe walls, evangelism limited to what has been compared to scalping expeditions into enemy territory for a few more trophies of conquest. That "enemy territory" is not an unconquered waste of the lost, doomed to damnation simply because no hunting expedition has yet arrived. The enemy, admittedly, still exists — a powerful prince of this world. But the victory over him has already been won. The distinction between those inside and those outside the church is not one between the saved and the lost, but between those who have heard the good news of the victory and those who are unaware of it.

Those whom a mistaken evangelism has been tempted to call the lost are, to employ an analogy, in the state of the slaves in the days of the American Civil War who had not yet heard of the Emancipation Proclamation. Their condition as slaves was still real enough. Masters could still, at worst, tyrannize over them with whip and lash. But their status as freemen was already won, and merely awaited the arrival of a herald of emancipation to become real in its turn. That the privilege of freedom could be refused — as freedom from conformity to this world can be refused — is, of course, a fact also. Many of the Children of Israel, freed from slavery under Pharaoh, found freedom a burden, and longed for the fleshpots of Egypt. The gospel is not one of a cheap universalism of salvation. At Judgment Day, "saved" and "lost" will not be idle words. Paul can speak of the "lost: in whom the god of this world hath blinded the minds of them which believe not" (II Cor. 4:3-4). But if our evangelism presumes to monopolize the word "saved" for ourselves, however generous we may be in welcoming properly qualified new recruits into our company, we may discover that judgment at the Great Assize will begin with the house of God. Withdrawal and separateness as an excuse for luxuriating in our safe harbors is nothing short of apostasy to our vocation.

Running alongside much of our contemporary rediscovery of the Biblical revelation of Christ's universal Lordship, and hence of the meaning of the gospel for the world as well as the church, is a parallel rediscovery of the world-affirming meaning of the drama of the incarnation itself. It seems at times as if this central event dogma of Christianity (never, of course, denied by the church) nevertheless lies buried for generations and needs periodic resurrection. Pages could be devoted to citations illustrating how pioneers of the church's mission to our historical era are finding in the incarnation fact the inspiration for a revolutionary evangelism — an evangelism not afraid of being accused of "worldliness." As an example of a New Testament scholar's underscoring the worldly "scandal" of the incarnation, note this paragraph from John Oman's *Grace and Personality:*

In the life of Jesus nothing is more conspicuous than his meager interest in specially sacred doings, and his profound interest in the most ordinary doings of the secular life. In his parables the only figures from the special religious life of a specially religious time are the Pharisee praying with himself in the Temple and the Priest and the Levite turning aside on the road to Jerusalem — self-approving and little-approved men, solitary to their heart's core. But what a varied secular procession of kings and slaves, bailiffs and debtors, and farmers and fisherfolk, and housewives, and children, and all at their secular occupations, with more feasting than fasting, and more marriages than funerals.[20]

George MacLeod, founder of the Iona Community and a pioneer of the "secular evangelism" of our time, issues a call for discipleship of this "worldly" Christ:

I am recovering the claim that Jesus was not crucified in a cathedral between two candles, but on a cross between two thieves; on a town garbage heap; at a crossroads so cosmopolitan that they had to write his title in Hebrew and in Latin and in Greek (or shall we say in English, in Bantu, and in Afrikaans?); at the kind of place where cynics talk smut and thieves curse and soldiers gamble. Because that is where he died. And that is what he died about. And that is where churchmen should be and what churchmen should be about.[21]

A fresh appreciation of the dogma of the incarnation is, however, not the only motivation for a revolution in the theology of evangelism. An equally powerful impulse to explore a re-orientation in understanding the church's mission to the world consists in a new look at the man to be evangelized in our era and the world in which this modern man now lives and acts.

The literature devoted to describing "modern" man is by now nothing short of enormous. Phrases such as "the organization man" or "the lonely crowd" are today common coin. We speak freely of communist man or technological man, of mass man or autonomous man. Theologians, in their turn, are contributing to such a verbal harvest. A good summary of this theological invasion of anthropological territory is R. Gregor Smith's *The New Man*.[22] Much of the volume consists of an analysis of the most daring novelty in this area of exploration, namely, the description of the man of our time as "religionless man," a phrase used by Dietrich Bonhoeffer. Also devoted to the stir in German theological circles which Bonhoeffer's provocative insights have evoked is a series of essays entitled *Die mündige Welt.*[23] The phrase suffers in translation, especially when the individual man, too, is spoken of as "*mündig.*" The best attempt is probably the paraphrase "the world come of age" and "man come of age." The analogy embodied in this phrase is helpful in winning an understanding of what Bonhoeffer and his followers are trying to tell us. The secularization of a once Christianized social order, so the argument runs, has progressed only by degrees. Until recently it stopped short at certain border lines, or "borders of existence." God was permitted to retain a sphere of rule and influence in crisis experiences or in a realm set apart and labeled "religion." He belongs "in church," but not in the world. Whether we can be won to an interest in this cultural specialty, today largely a middle-class preserve or "ghetto," is left to voluntary choice. We can participate in church activities or we can leave them alone. Real life goes on outside church walls. Man was for long, so it seems, still an adolescent and felt the need of running to "mother church" for help in crisis situations — birth, sickness, death. But man is come of age now, mature, and no longer in need of religion as a crutch. Machines run without divine intervention. A broken spindle is not healed by prayer, nor does modern industry expect miracles to happen to save it from recessions or bankruptcy.

But let Bonhoeffer speak for himself. The quotation comes from his *Prisoner for God: Letters and Papers from Prison,* letters written when, having participated in the assassination plot against Hitler, and the plot having failed, he awaited execution in a prison camp.

Religious people speak of God when human perception is (often just from laziness) at an end, or human resources fail: it is really always the *deus ex machina* they call to their aid, either for the so-called solving of insoluble problems or as support in human failure — always, that is to say, helping out human weakness or on the borders of human existence. Of necessity that can only go on until men can, by their own strength, push those borders back a little farther, so that God becomes superfluous as a *deus ex machina.* I

have come to be doubtful even about talking of "borders of existence." Is even death, since men are scarcely afraid of it anymore,
and sin, which they scarcely understand anymore, still a genuine
border line? It always seems to me that in talking thus we are only
seeking frantically to make room for God. I should like to speak of
God not on the borders of life, but at its center, not in weakness, but
in strength, not therefore, in man's suffering and death, but in his
life and prosperity. . . . God is the "beyond" in the midst of life.
The church stands not where human powers give out, on the borders, but in the center of the village.[24]

The issue raised by this revolutionary young theologian is
so important that it warrants the inclusion here of another excerpt from his correspondence — a passage receiving in our
day the honor of frequent citation:

During the last year or so I have come to appreciate the "worldliness" of Christianity as never before. The Christian is not a *homo
religiosus*, but a man, pure and simple, just as Jesus was a man, compared with John the Baptist anyhow. I don't mean the shallow this-
worldliness of the enlightened, the busy, the comfortable, or the
lascivious. It is something more profound than that, something in
which the knowledge of death and resurrection is ever present. I
believe Luther lived a this-worldly life in this sense. . . . It is only
by living completely in this world that one learns to believe. One
must abandon every attempt to make something of oneself, whether
it be saint or sinner, churchman (the priestly type, so-called!), a
righteous man or an unrighteous one, a sick man or a healthy one.
This is what I mean by worldliness — taking life in one's stride, with
all its duties and problems, its successes and failures, its experiences
and helplessness. It is in such a life that we can throw ourselves
utterly into the hands of God and participate in his sufferings in the
world and watch with Christ in Gethsemane. . . . How can success make us arrogant, or failure lead us astray, when we participate
in the sufferings of God by living in the world?[25]

"We are proceeding," so Bonhoeffer summarizes his analysis
of our age, "toward a time of no religion at all; men as they
are now cannot be religious anymore." And he asks the crucial
question: "How can Christ become Lord even of those with no

religion? What is the significance of the church in a religionless world? " [26]

Now it is dangerous to erect a full doctrinal structure on insights which, however passionately held, express only one facet of the experience and convictions of this martyred Christian. *Prisoner for God* must be read in conjunction with his *The Cost of Discipleship*, as also his early book on the church, *Sanctorum Communio*, and, most importantly, his later work descriptive of the Christian communal life when separated *from* the world and when it nurtures its own existence, *Life Together*.[27] Viewed in perspective, Bonhoeffer's " worldly Christianity " is no plea for liquidating the church and permitting " religionless " secularism to take over. But it takes seriously the call to the church, which he defines as " Christ in community," to follow its Lord where he walked and where he was crucified — in the secular world. More than one Bonhoeffer disciple has called attention to the fact that the Jesus of the Gospels did not remain in the Temple waiting for people to come to him for instruction.

It is only fair, furthermore, to note that even loyal disciples of Bonhoeffer (and these are multiplying rapidly) are prepared to supply corrective footnotes to his provocative analysis of the " new man " of our time. I venture to join their company. His use of the phrase " religionless man," for example, ignores half of the paradox inherent in the word " religion." Autonomous, secular man is still " responsible man," and this involves him in the necessity to find a god to worship, or, to use Tillich's phrase, some " ultimate concern." At the very least, he is responsible to himself. He becomes his own god and his own idol-worshiper. He has not escaped the life of " care," or of anxiety, or of what Kierkegaard honors with the emphatic word " dread." Bonhoeffer may be right in his assertion that modern man no longer fears physical death. Even the ancient Stoics made of suicide a kind of welcomed last sacrament. But modern man is a victim still of the tragedy of time, and of the panic of closing doors — growing old, ambition's failures, and the tyranny of social conformity. He is still, to use the language of Paul, "under the law." His conscience informs him that he is facing daily and hourly a prosecutor in a courtroom, even though he may think that he can choose his own judge, or bribe the One on the throne.

Theologians who are taking seriously the call to a worldly Christianity agree that Bonhoeffer leaves his own question, "How can Christ become Lord even of those with no religion?" unanswered. This may be a task for our generation. One clue may be found in the fact just noted that the secular world and life within it exist under the law and under judgment just as much as do the church and "religion." Here the other side of the paradox hidden in the word "religion" can come into its own. Religion, as suggested earlier, can serve as a way of avoiding an interview with the real God, but life in the world cannot thus serve as an escape. Here is no contemplative retreat, no opportunity for withdrawal from conflict and decision. Here life is inescapably *eschatological* — a word that Christian communication will simply have to domesticate and bring into the realm of common speech. Every step into the future is eschatological — a hint of some kind of summing up of past and present and the risking of a destiny. The intuition that this destiny might involve someday an ultimate summing up ("This night your soul is required of you") has not been a universal belief of mankind for nothing.

"Do you not know," asks Kierkegaard, "that there comes a midnight hour when everyone has to throw off his mask? Do you think you can slip away a little before midnight in order to avoid this? Or are you not terrified by it?" [28] Few men and women of our time, mature and "come of age" as they may pretend to be, can hear such a warning without a touch of adolescent fear. The picturization of the Judge "coming on the clouds of heaven" bequeathed to us in our New Testament may deserve some remythologizing. Nevertheless, the reality symbolized by this vision casts a daily foretaste of judgment into our lives.

"Man come of age" in our time may be able to avoid religion — at least *our* religion, *our* church, *our* preaching of the gospel. But he cannot avoid God. He lives under the law and under judgment. So do *we!* At the final summing up of history our religion may help us not one bit. We may be in a worse state than our religionless neighbor. And this neighbor of ours often senses this. That is why he is tempted to despise our religious superiority parades, our ghettos of middle-class respectability, our avoidance of fellowship with his kind. But could he so easily have despised the Christ of the Palestine roads? Will he despise us if we can take discipleship of Christ seriously and, as Bonhoeffer pleads, "participate in Christ's sufferings in the world"? Bonhoeffer may be right when he says that "it is only by living completely in this world that one learns to believe." We shall learn to accept the religionless man as fully our neighbor and to walk a second mile with him on the pathway of his choosing.

To speak of worldly holiness or holy worldliness might have shocked our pietistic grandfathers or a Roman Catholic of an earlier generation. It is ceasing to shock today, and nowhere less, so it seems, than in the powerful lay movements in Roman Catholicism itself. The Roman Catholic concept of sainthood is no longer a monopoly of the cloister, and an apostolate of the laity is on the march. Non-Roman Christianity can learn much from these stirrings in the inheritor of medieval Christendom. Bonhoeffer and his followers are not alone in rediscovering incarnational evangelism.

The implications of this secular evangelism for a Christian style of life for our time, however, especially as this involves the laity, must await later treatment. In the meantime, one further important insight into the strange mystery of religionless or secular man deserves attention — one that can serve as an introduction to the next chapter.

Religionless, or secular, or autonomous man — the adjectives are to some extent synonymous — is under the illusion that he is emancipated from the rule of a power above his creating. He

lives in a one-story universe. The three-story universe —
heaven, earth, and hell — in which his grandfathers found
themselves at home, even when they revolted against its Ruler,
has vanished into the realm of poetry and tales for children.
In calling attention to this undoubted change in our cos-
mological environment, Rudolf Bultmann has served us well,
however tentatively we may be willing to receive his recon-
structions. Ours is, by way of contrast to the world of our
grandfathers, a strange, new world. For it Nietzsche's assertion
that "God is dead" seems at times to have come true. But if
God has apparently removed himself and has left the world
now to autonomous man, man as his own neighbor has not
vanished. Adolescent man felt himself threatened by higher
powers, demonic and divine. The New Man feels himself
threatened by his fellowman. A pioneer evangelist of our time,
Horst Symanowski, familiar with the religionless working class
of Germany, describes the contrast vividly. In the era of Christendom, before the arrival of the New Man, the basic problem
confronting religious man was:

"How can I find a gracious God?" This question drove men to
search desperately for an answer. It was the motor for their action
in the world; it unleashed crusades and wars. This cry robbed them
of sleep. Do many men today lie awake in order to find an answer
to this question? It does not disturb our sleep. We no longer ask this
question, or we label it antiquated. But a different question haunts
us also. It agitates entire nations. It makes us in our turn victims of
anxiety and despair. How can I find a gracious neighbor? How can
we still somehow live at peace with one another? [29]

Such a narrowing down of the religious question of our
time (I use the word "religion" boldly once more) may partake of exaggeration. In "border situations," other questions
involving other tokens of dread are certainly still alive. Yet the
writer just cited does call attention to a fact that does not admit
of doubt. Modern man has not solved the problem of "the
neighbor." Here even autonomous man meets the limit of his
lordly role. Here he encounters what Bonhoeffer calls "the

Transcendent." And it may be that only as he confronts the full implications of making his peace with this Transcendent may he be led to accepting a confrontation with the ultimate Transcendent — God.

As we, accordingly, seek ways and means of making the gospel relevant to modern secular man, what might be called the "theology of the neighbor" may become very important. It is startling in its implications, and we may be only in the beginning of exploring its depths. One of the basic concepts of the Bible, as already suggested, looms on the horizon at once — the law. Religionless man may be under the illusion that "God is dead," but his neighbor is always a living reality. And in meeting his neighbor, he confronts the law. In confronting the law, whether he admits this or not, he is in dialogue with the Creator of law. "God's law," so a contemporary Swedish theologian voices this insight, "is present with us in the world because our neighbor is. As soon as a fellowman comes on the scene, law comes on the scene: an order is heard, the Creator of the world speaks and gives command." [30]

A meeting of a Christian with his neighbor, in turn, is a meeting with Christ — or, at least, an invitation to see in that neighbor Christ's call to share in his cross and resurrection. Has any of us ever taken with full seriousness the Judgment scene in which the Lord identifies himself with even the lowliest neighbor we shall ever meet? We hear the words: "Truly, I say to you, as you did it to one of the least of these my brethren, you did it to me" (Matt. 25:40). If this is true, the time might come when the neighbor, from his side, could see Christ in our act of discipleship.[31]

We can listen with profit, accordingly, to Horst Symanowski as he pleads the cause of incarnational evangelism. It is as "neighbor" that Christ can make his first contact with man in our secularized Western world. The very heart of the gospel of the incarnation is that Christ became our neighbor. This must become also the heart of Christian witness in our time. "He is among us! He does not wish to be found by way of climbing a religious ladder reaching into the unknown, but he walks with us on our human plane." [32]

The communication of the gospel to modern man, in other words, if we follow the clue of our cited pioneers, may have to begin where contact with secular man is still possible — giving him an answer to his question: " How can I find a gracious neighbor? " How can we still live with one another — husband with wife, parents with children, employer with employee? This descent, as it were, to the horizontal plane may prove to be dangerous business. It may look as if God " who is in heaven " were ignored and only man in his one-story universe were left. But if we trust fully the good news of the incarnation, we shall not be alone on the horizontal plane. Christ will be with us. And we have his assurance that " he who has seen me has seen the Father " (John 14:9). " No man has ever seen God. . . . If any one says, ' I love God,' and hates his brother, he is a liar; for he who does not love his brother whom he has seen, cannot love God whom he has not seen." (I John 4:12, 20.)

One of the great word symbols of the New Testament can loom large on our horizon now — the word " reconciliation." Only as neighbor is reconciled with neighbor can men learn again to live with one another. The gospel entrusted to us receives in the New Testament many glorious summations. For our time one of the most important may be that it is the " message of reconciliation." " God was in Christ reconciling the world to himself, . . . and entrusting to us the message of reconciliation." (II Cor. 5:19.)

What is involved in communicating the gospel as a message of reconciliation between man and man and man with God will be the theme of the next chapters.

Chapter II

"Hell Is Other People"

How can we still live with one another? How or where shall I find a gracious neighbor? These questions came to the fore as we looked at modern man in his strange, new world. Christianity must carry its message to men where they are. One of man's basic needs today is a gospel of reconciliation between himself and his fellowman. What is the relevance of the God of the Christian faith to this deep hunger?

When we examine the texts in the New Testament in which the ministry of reconciliation is brought to our attention, it becomes obvious that this ministry has, first of all, a vertical dimension in mind — the gospel of God's "reconciling the world to himself, not counting their trespasses against them," God "making peace by the blood of his cross, . . . to reconcile to himself all things" (II Cor. 5:19; Col. 1:20). To love God retains its rank as the first and great commandment. But there is a second, love of neighbor. And its likeness to the first is commandment also, a fact that may be especially important for our time.

"If we love one another, God abides in us and his love is perfected in us." (I John 4:12.) Even the Lord's Prayer and the Sermon on the Mount weave together reconciliation with the Father and with our neighbor. "If you are offering your gift at the altar," so we recall the familiar words of the Sermon, "and there remember that your brother has something against you, leave your gift there before the altar and go; first be reconciled to your brother, and then come and offer your gift." (Matt. 5:23-24.) Our pioneers in evangelism may be reminding us that this precept is meant for the church and its evangelizing ministry as well as for the individual. Have our brothers in the religionless world nothing against us? Do we easily obey the command to go and be reconciled with them — and *then* enter our sanctuaries? To " go to church " is frequently easy enough. To go into the neighboring slum is hard!

It would, of course, be a tragic misunderstanding if the appeal to worldly holiness resulted in the neglect of the corporate life of the witnessing community. The ministry of reconciliation implies a ministering agency. Christ present in his world means " Christ existing in community " — Bonhoeffer's favorite definition of the church in the world.

An evangelizing ministry " in the world," however, soon experiences the loneliness of leaving the safety of the sanctuary and risking the dangers of the open road. It is as if God must be left behind for a time to take care of himself in his temple. How tempting it is to depend upon the temple to do its own evangelizing or to limit the evangelizing effort to an invitation into the sanctuary where God can take over. The very concept of evangelism has become impoverished by having become synonymous frequently with mere church attendance recruitment. " Bring a friend with you to church." " We invite you to our friendly fellowship." These are phrases with which evangelism campaigns are familiar. Nor are they to be judged as if they were on the level of Madison Avenue advertising schemes. Many an outsider has had his first contact with the gospel precisely " in the church." " Fellowship evangelism " if the phrase be permitted, may, indeed, be one of the most effective means of welcoming the stranger to his Heavenly Father's household. He may have to experience grace in the form of such simple welcome into a Christian family environment before the story of the family's founding in a drama of a cross and a resurrection can have any meaning. The witnessing power of the body of Christ is one of the foci in the ellipse of

any evangelizing ministry and need not be belittled by pleading for an equal emphasis on the call for evangelism freed from
even the highest ulterior motive. It will, in fact, receive further
attention later.

At this point it is needful, however, to call attention to its
dangers when it serves as an escape from the more demanding
vocation to meet our neighbor before he has found his way
into the church. " Let the minister take over after we have rec-
ommended church attendance." How easy this is compared
with the full demand of witnessing as a Christian in the world!
The outsider is often quick to suspect an ulterior motive in our
sales rhetoric for our church around the corner: " If we so
much as step inside its doors, a solicitor for a contribution to
its parish budget will ring our doorbell the next day." Is the
outsider wholly wrong in thus frequently equating our evangelism with propaganda in behalf of an institution in need of
support in place of an invitation to partake of the free grace
of God's love? " Ho, every one who thirsts, come to the waters;
and he who has no money, come, buy and eat! " (Isa. 55:1.)
Our Lord may have had such true evangelism in mind as a
contrast to what he condemns in no uncertain terms as self-
centered proselytism: " Woe to you, scribes and Pharisees,
hypocrites! for you traverse sea and land to make a single
proselyte, and when he becomes a proselyte, you make him
twice as much a child of hell as yourselves " (Matt. 23:15).
Such words, we say, cannot possibly apply to us! Yet many an
outwardly prosperous congregation would find it profitable to
take our Lord's indictment quite seriously. Proselytism, when it
denotes a hunting expedition for new supporters of a church's
institutional prosperity, can easily turn into the very opposite
of true evangelism.

One proof of the fact that the distinction between true evangelism and proselytism is one of more than academic interest
could well be a realistic look at what has happened, on the
American scene at least, to the very concept of a parish. The
term " parish " once meant — and still does in much of Europe

and in Roman Catholic ecclesiology — a geographical area for
which a church with its clergy assumed responsibility. Professing Christians within its boundaries constituted the congregation. Residents who were not professing Christians were, however, no less the concern of the evangelizing agency which God
had set up in the midst of the area. Members of the congregation did not choose who might be their neighbors at worship.
They worshiped with neighbors whom God in a sense had
chosen for them. Unless the parish as a neighborhood had itself
become a caste enclave, a little at least of Paul's description
could receive manifestation: " Here there cannot be Greek and
Jew, circumcised and uncircumcised, barbarian, Scythian,
slave, free man, but Christ is all, and in all " (Col. 3:11). There
are many reasons why the boundary parish has not maintained
itself in our urban and suburban environment. Nor is our
substitution of congregational for parish church life in all respects harmful. Yet it is a glaring fact, surely, that the very
concept of a church's evangelizing ministry as one directed
first of all to winning for life within the body of Christ the
neighbors God has given us has been replaced by what a recent
observer has termed evangelism by co-optation.[33]

Our ideal is a congregation made up of those who are already our friends, those who, as we say, " will be happy in our
fellowship." We leave uncongenial neighbors, though they
may be living next door, for some other congregation's evangelizing. Is proselytism too strong a word to describe some at
least of our evangelistic campaigns?

Leaving for later treatment the role of the gathered church
as itself an agency of gospel witness, the hard truth remains
that it is on the open roads of everyday life outside church
walls where Christ as Reconciler may be able to speak his first
word. The disciple of Christ, in turn, cannot delay his reconciling ministry until the burden of witnessing can be neatly
referred to the ordained clergyman or even to the appeal of
formalized worship. We are to be bearers of Christ's ministry
of caring in shop and factory, in daily work and play, as well

as in our protected church enclaves. Such is God's own evangelism; and the letter to the Ephesians tells us that we are to be "imitators of God" (ch. 5:1). The God we are to imitate does not limit his outgoing love to those who have honored him by church attendance. He too leaves his temple and seeks the lost on the highways of the world. "He makes his sun rise on the evil and on the good, and sends rain on the just and on the unjust." (Matt. 5:45.) "While we were yet sinners Christ died for us." (Rom. 5:8.)

Every pastor of a flock can testify that calls for a ministry of reconciliation on the human plane crowd upon him. Husbands are estranged from wives, wives from husbands, children from father or mother, neighbor from neighbor. Widen the horizon to include the world of industry or politics, and the need for a gospel of reconciliation between man and man takes on global proportions. Unless the church can become relevant to this hunger for "grace" on the plane of our human interpersonal relations, it looks, even to the layman still faithful to his pilgrimage to his pew on Sunday mornings, like an irrelevant museum of antiquities. The commandment to love God with soul and mind and strength may be accorded some sort of priority, but the commandment to love our neighbor has priority in practical interpretations of what religion is all about.

This demand on the part of both those inside and outside the churches to see the relevancy of the gospel on the horizontal plane must, indeed, be taken seriously. Christ, as already hinted, may have to meet them as "neighbor" before he can win their allegiance as Lord. Every Christian, in Luther's phrase, is called to become Christ to his neighbor. A warning, however, should be voiced at once. Every Christian is called to an imitation of Christ on the horizontal plane of man's life alongside his neighbor. This is, indeed, the scene for many a first encounter between an outsider and the grace of God. But woe unto the Christian witness if he is under the illusion that he can himself play the role of Savior. He dare not even assume the right to become his neighbor's conscience. The neighbor must be left free to meet Christ for himself. The witness must remain aware of a further fact. Christ's becoming our neighbor — as one who ate with publicans and sinners — was not the end of his ministry. Nor must it be the end of our witnessing. Christ came down from heaven to share our human lot. That is glorious good news. But he came not only to share our human lot: he came to redeem it on a cross. Dangers can lie in wait for all incarnational evangelism if it stops short of loyalty to a theology of the atonement. Man's need for grace may reveal itself first on the horizontal plane of our human interpersonal relations, but the need does not supply the answer. The answer involves the vertical relation with the risen and ascended Christ and not merely with the Jesus of the Palestine roads.

For if the answer is looked for on the horizontal plane alone, Christianity confronts in our time rivals of gigantic power. It is on this plane that it must prove its right to be heard. But it will deserve defeat if the salvation it offers is dependent on human resources alone, even those of Christian brotherhood. Man's need, in its real dimension, must be revealed as a cry for God — for Christ as Savior as well as Neighbor.

The most obvious rival to Christianity as it, too, offers an answer to man's cry for help in his interpersonal relationships is today familiar to all. I need not burden these pages with an exposition of the gospel according to Karl Marx, but it behooves us as Christians to see why it wins the hearts of men in our religionless era. I doubt that the Scriptural word " reconciliation " plays a great role in communist literature, but clearly a secularized version of it animates Marxist mystique — love of man for man's sake. Exorcise from this Marxist dogma its dependence on sheer power by way of a dictatorship of the proletariat, and the gospel of love of man for man's sake has its devotees in our still democratic society also. We call it humanism. On our side of the Iron Curtain it no longer marches under the banner of a naïve hope for a utopia just around the corner, but it is by no means dead or ready for a quick conversion to Christianity. It can still present a twofold appeal, especially to the young — emancipation from the tyranny of " Sunday school religion " and, as substitute, the worship of heroic ideals. By way of illustration, I venture to cite its creed in the form of a moving poem — Thomas Hardy's *A Plaint to Man*. A " fictional " god is the speaker:

> When you slowly emerged from the den of Time,
>   And gained percipience as you grew,
> And fleshed you fair out of shapeless slime,
>
> Wherefore, O Man, did there come to you
>   The unhappy need of creating me —
> A form like your own — for praying to?
>
> My Virtue, power, utility,
>   Within my maker must all abide,
> Since none in myself can ever be,
>
> One thin as a phasm on a lantern slide
>   Shown forth in the dark upon some dim sheet,
> And by none but its showman vivified.
>
> " Such a forced device," you may say, " is meet
>   For easing a loaded heart at whiles:
> Man needs to conceive of a mercy seat
>
> " Somewhere above the gloomy aisles
>   Of this wailful world, or he could not bear
> The irk no local hope beguiles."
>
> But since I was framed in your first despair
>   The doing without me has had no play
> In the minds of men when shadows scare;
>
> And now that I dwindle day by day
>   Beside the deicide eyes of seers
> In a light that will not let me stay,
>
> And tomorrow the whole of me disappears,
>   The truth should be told, and the fact be faced
> That had best been faced in earlier years:
>
> The fact of life with dependence placed
>   On the human heart's resource alone
> In brotherhood bonded close and graced

> With loving-kindness fully blown,
> And visioned help unsought, unknown.[34]

In slightly modified form, a gospel of love of man for man's sake may have found a comfortable home within many of our churches themselves. Once more I spare the reader a long description of what, in theological discourse, has come to be called liberal, or perhaps more accurately humanist, Christianity. This version of Christianity did not find it too difficult to garner from the Bible a rich harvest of moral ideals. The Jesus of the Gospel story could be honored as teacher and hero, the Sermon on the Mount a blueprint of the goal for a brotherhood of man. If the observers of the shape of religion in America cited in the previous chapter are right in defining this shape as "religion in general," this can best be understood as precisely a syncretistic moral idealism — a religion short-circuiting the divisiveness of confessions and creeds, a religion virtually without theology. And that means, in final analysis, religion without God. We remain in a one-story universe, man his own savior.

I have used the phrase "love of man for man's sake" to describe one aspect at least of what may already have emerged as the most obvious rival to Christianity in our time. Man's need for grace, as we try to live with one another, is to be answered on the horizontal plane where the need itself has become acute. I wonder whether those of us not yet exiled in a religionless world realize how powerful an appeal this rival gospel can address to the men and women of our time. Compared with it, Christianity, seen as merely sentimentality and otherworldliness, must frequently appear weak and anemic, truly opium for the people. The Christian, as many an outsider sees him, obeys the call of the psalmist (Ps. 55:22) to cast his burden on the Lord, concentrates his attention on his individual salvation, and imprisons his piety within the four walls of his church. By way of contrast, a religion of human brotherhood — love of fellowman now, in place of love of a distant deity — despises such cowardly escape from humanity's burden of mutual care and fellowship in the encounter with fate.

A Roman Catholic author expresses this paradox vividly. The quotation appears in a discussion of the initial handicap burdening Christianity when it wishes to compete with the newly arising secular gospels of a socialist humanism in which concern for man and his earthly happiness is the center of attention. The author identifies herself with the Christian community and contrasts it with its secular rivals:

The love of man for man's sake must necessarily be stronger and richer in other camps than ours. Are they not confined within a world from which heaven has been removed like a roof? On the level floor of a plain visible from end to end, objects stand out stark and bare, hopeless captives of the relentless light which has stripped them of every wonder, every blessed dream. And on such an earth, without cover or distance, when longing reaches into the void, these people are packed unendurably tight, treading on each other's feet, too close to escape. These people, who have nothing but themselves, who are without God, how terribly important they must become to one another — important as we who live simultaneously and inseparably with God can never be important to each other.[35]

The hunger for community, for brotherhood, for some form of communism, if we can steal the word from the Marxist scriptures, for some alleviation of man's loneliness and his nakedness in the face of fate and death — this, surely, is deeply implanted in the human heart. What is more tempting than to look to a fellowman for a savior? Is not fraternity a natural endowment of communal humanity? Nor indeed can we deny even to fallen humanity the ministry of what has been called " natural grace." "God setteth the solitary in families." Husbands loved their wives, and wives loved their husbands even before the advent of the Christian church. Our Lord drew material for his parables from this same fallen human nature, reminding his hearers that even those who are evil know how to give good gifts to their children (Luke 11:13). Friendships are not monopolies of Christians, nor at least a partial surrender of self-centeredness to man-made fellowships — clubs, sodalities, labor unions, managerial associations, or any of the hundreds of communal groupings that win our allegiance and trust. There is even such a thing as honor among thieves. And we have seen in our time the demonic power for human unification of shared hatred — the Nazi mass meeting and the proletariat revolt against the citadels of privilege. Anyone who ever hears the "Internationale" sung by an army of marching men will be amazed as he witnesses the force for creating a communal one "out of many" latent in unredeemed human nature.

Gratitude is proper for such ministrations of natural grace. Many of these secular alleviations of our loneliness can become analogies for the fellowship of the Holy Spirit. Many, in our Western lands which once constituted Christendom, are still beneficiaries of Christian grace. Could Alcoholics Anonymous, for example, be conceivable in pagan Rome? The question could be asked whether this redeeming brotherhood could exist in atheist Russia.

Is there, then, if "natural grace" is accorded full cultivation, still need of a ministry of reconciliation that brings God upon the scene? As already hinted, some at least of the manifestations of fraternity still left in our world are living on borrowed, though often unacknowledged, power inherited from our Christian past. Remove this still-latent grace of Christianity, however, from our world and leave it to the rule of naked atheism, and could these analogies of fraternity long continue? They are, insofar as they exist on their own, illustrations of "natural religion." Their worship is ultimately a worship of idols. The Bible has much to say about idolatry — much that is relevant to our time. An idol dies when it is no longer supplied with food by its worshipers. In final testing it fails to save its devotees. It has feet of clay.

In an earlier paragraph I hinted at the fact that the religion of love of man for man's sake, usually called humanism, is facing today a crisis of disillusionment. Confessions of this loss of nerve are multiplying all about us and may well deserve our attention. By way of paradoxical result, they may win a hearing for the gospel. Even when the gospel is not accepted, it will no longer be judged irrelevant.

It comes as a shock to many pious people to be told that some of our best theologians today are our atheist philosophers, playwrights, and poets. Yet such a claim can be at least partially validated. To catch a fresh grasp upon the meaning of life under grace, it may indeed be helpful to see human existence without grace. " Human life without grace " — the phrase may seem puzzling at first. As a citation from a contemporary observer in the previous chapter argued, the word " grace " itself has lost all meaning even for many professing Christians. But this handicap does not apply to the word symbol describing the opposite of grace, namely, " disgrace." We employ it freely in common speech. A failing schoolboy is in disgrace with his teacher. A husband disloyal to his marriage vows is in disgrace with his wife. A relationship has been broken. Alienation and loneliness are the result. An island of isolation has appeared. The experience of such life without grace can throw light on what its opposite might mean, namely, grace as a gift of reunion. The word " gift " is used advisedly. Anyone experiencing the pain of disgrace is surely made aware that he cannot by himself manipulate the healing of a broken relationship. Healing must come by way of precisely an unearned gift.

Such a clarification of what the phrase " life without grace " can signify may serve as an introduction to illustrations of its depth dimensions. Some of the most powerful portrayals of man on his own in a godless world are ready to hand today in current existentialist literature.

I choose for examples two excerpts from the writings of the most famous, or at least the most notable, atheist philosopher of our generation, Jean-Paul Sartre. Here is a capsule summary of his analysis of human existence without God:

Man can do nothing unless he first understands that he must count on no one but himself, that he is alone, abandoned on earth in the midst of his infinite responsibilities, without help, with no other aims than the ones he sets for himself on this earth. . . . Life is absurd, love is impossible. There is no way of knowing the true meaning of what we are doing. Perhaps our actions have no meaning.[36]

My second excerpt — only a phrase — is taken from Sartre's drama *No Exit*. This play has received much discussion of late, an indication that it speaks to our condition as we know it in our time. Hence even repetitive allusion may be pardoned. Like any honest atheist, Sartre cannot avoid theological symbols. He must employ the terminology of the religion against which his disbelief is directed. Sartre chooses as setting for his drama the hell of religious eschatology. Three characters find themselves in a room which they gradually realize is to be their lodging for eternity. Each has a guilt-laden past. Gradually the three characters reveal their past histories to one another even when they realize that this results in mutual loathing. "Hell is other people," so reads the most famous line of the play. Yet when the door flies open and they can leave their torture chamber, they refuse freedom. Each needs the others whom he hates. Loneliness and the fear of not being recognized as a person even in a relationship of mutual hatred and disgust would be worse than community in damnation. Each needs the others as an audience for self-justification. What a reader of the play does not always notice, yet what is perhaps of equal importance with the phrase " Hell is other people," is the fact that the characters have no eyelids. Theirs is a sleepless world. There is nothing to hope for except that which they can win for themselves, and in such a never-ending struggle there is no time for sleep. To relax even for a moment might mean surrender of self-justification. They would stand at the brink of a frightening void.

Is this an exaggerated picture of the religionless world of our time? I think not, though most of us are still taking our Christianized common life so much for granted that we do not see the hell beneath the thin crust of mere human brotherhood.

This hell, however, is revealing itself all around us. We are, all of us, often in its forecourts ourselves. Why, for example, is our age called the Age of Anxiety? Is it not because self-justification demands sleepless care? We are careful about our every move and word — anxious to do the right thing so as to be accepted by " other people." It is precisely " other people " who induce this care.[37] Not for a moment dare we forget ourselves. Our salvation from turning into a social cipher, a nonentity no longer recognized as a person, is an endless striving, to employ the language of Paul, for " justification by works alone." We do not dare to be careless. That might mean risking our very selves to a feared unknown. The Bible will call this feared unknown " the grace of God " and the way to it " justification by grace through faith." But for this we are not prepared, since it implies the surrender of the very self which has demanded our endless care.[38]

It will be seen that I have already called into dialogue the insights of the Bible. But before these can be given full right of witness, a further analysis of our human state may be in order.

" Hell is other people," says Sartre. We may shrink from quite so bold a picture of what a realistic diagnosis of our common life might reveal. We still trust the illusions of natural religion. But let us dare to look again beneath the surface of our human togetherness. I might begin with a saying of Pascal's, the Christian " moralist " of the seventeenth century: " I set it down as a fact that if all men knew what each said of the other, there would not be four friends in this world." [39] A ruthless look into the mirror of conscience will lead all of us to an acceptance of the truth of Pascal's insight. We all wear masks. Keeping them in repair is the cause of our carefulness and our insomnia. Remove these masks? We would not dare. Even our nearest and dearest would not endure the sight. We cannot endure the sight ourselves. Any psychiatrist could testify to the enormous resistance of his patients to even a little self-exposure. An allusion to only one of the seven deadly sins,

that of jealousy, can bring visions to every one of us of the
deep chasm of alienation separating us from even beloved
friends, let alone casual neighbors. Who of us could not see
himself described in Shakespeare's sonnet on envy (Sonnet 29)?

> When in disgrace with fortune and men's eyes
>   I all alone bewail my outcaste state,
> And trouble deaf heaven with my bootless cries,
>   And look upon myself and curse my fate,
> Wishing me like to one more rich in hope,
>   Featur'd like him, like him with friends possess'd
> Desiring this man's art and that man's scope,
>   With what I most enjoy contented least

We note Shakespeare's use of the word "disgrace." We note,
too, the matchless diagnosis of its resultant penalties in the
form of loneliness and life as an outcast. The word "bewail,"
in turn, calls to mind one of the words of Jesus describing the
fate of those who refuse God's grace as one of wailing and
gnashing of teeth (Matt. 8:12). We may on occasion be
shocked to meet a warning of "hell fire" even in our Lord's
Sermon on the Mount (Matt. 5:22). Yet the experience of the
"hell of disgrace" — foretaste of a possible ultimate destiny —
which is surely not limited to isolated bad people, can bring
a wholesome fear into all our lives.

Another somewhat pictorial way of illustrating the profound
problem of reconciliation between man and man and the pow-
erlessness of mere human goodwill or natural religion to solve
the problem can be found in what could be called a space
analogy. A contemporary theologian, Karl Heim, has dealt at
some length with this analogy, though Sartre uses it also.

"My mind to me a kingdom is," says the poet. Your mind is
to you a kingdom as well. And these are rival kingdoms. Picture them for a moment as they are experienced subjectively.
Each is an almost limitless universe of memory and imagina-
tion. Each has a king ruling in the kingdom's citadel but free
to move within its borders. A meeting takes place with a neigh-

bor. Two space worlds collide. What will be the result? Will they immediately merge? Or is not the first impact one of conflict? I must surrender an area of my subjective kingdom to my neighbor or he must surrender an area to me. Who will speak first? How shall I reply? If it is a simple meeting on a street corner in which we gossip about sports or the weather, conflict is, of course, at a minimum. The meeting resembles fraternization in no-man's-land on the part of armies still at war. But when deeper issues are involved, surrender of royal rule on the part of one of the parties in the dialogue is inevitable. Both cannot talk at once. Listening comes hard. Many a conversation is a monologue duel, the opposite of what Martin Buber calls " the sacrament of dialogue."

Sartre, speaking in the first person, describes a meeting with a neighbor in a vivid phrase: " He has stolen my world away from me." [40] Sartre's grim picture may look overdrawn. Our need for recognition and fellowship may be so strong that even kingdom clashings may be welcomed. Boredom and life on an isolated island of loneliness are worse than fellowship even in hell. Almost any cocktail bar can illustrate this pitiful paradox. A character in T. S. Eliot's *The Cocktail Party* describes our universal experience of loneliness in a moving confession:

> No, it isn't that I want to be alone
> But everyone's alone — or so it seems to me.
> They make noises, and think they are talking to each other,
> They make faces, and think they understand each other,
> And I am sure they don't. Is that a delusion? [41]

Karl Heim's analysis of our space-world isolation is also worthy of citation:

The structure of the nonobjective space, in which we ego-beings coexist, is such as to give rise to that underlying conflict, which, once it is projected onto the plane of objectivity, transforms the whole world into a battlefield. This conflict follows from the mutually exclusive claims of the I and the Thou. Either I, Subject A, am the central pivot of the world, or else you, Subject B, are that center. . . . If we visualize this general conception of reality, reality appears to us as an immensely wide plain over which there lowers a dark, ominous storm cloud. From this storm cloud, which is charged with electricity, lightning flashes down incessantly. The countless beings which inhabit the plain wander across the broad expanse like fugitives, each by itself, homeless and restless, continually threatened by the lightning flashes, to which they are exposed every step of the way.[42]

What emerges from a realistic portrayal of human existence when man is on his own — man without God — can serve as backdrop to the good news of the gospel, the true message of reconciliation. But for this message we must go to the Bible and listen with new wonder and amazement to the story of the incarnation, the cross, and the resurrection, and of the new life of the people of God in Christ.

Chapter III

Redeeming Grace

If we turn now to Christianity for enlightenment on the problem of reconciling man and man, what do we find? Will it give the lie to the grim picture of our human existence, of hell as other people, which our ruthless existentialists have set before us? May not an optimistic view of man as by nature a child of a loving Creator and Father replace the pessimistic portrait just subjected to review?

If an easy solution to the problem of reconciliation between man and his neighbor is looked for in the Bible, grievous disappointment awaits us. Much preaching in the era of " liberal " or " humanist " Christianity (alluded to in the previous chapter) was under the illusion that a fairly easy solution was indeed in sight. Man, even imperfect or " fallen " man, had surely retained powers for achieving the good life if only these innate powers, so it was thought, could be aroused. Is not the Bible a veritable textbook of moral heroism — not least the incomparable biography of Christianity's founder? Are not appeals for ethical striving and the fulfillment of the commandment to love our neighbor to be found on almost every page of Holy Scripture? Let us present these winsomely enough as ideals and goals and the result must be an emerging Kingdom of God in which brotherhood will be on obvious display for all to see.

I speak with some critical animus on this topic because, in my vocation as a kind of professor of homiletics in a postgraduate clergy training institute, I have listened to scores of sermons which, whether the preacher intended this or not, nevertheless fell into the trap of witnessing to a gospel of mere natural religion. The command to love our neighbor as ourselves, and the implications of this command for our personal and social life loom large on our homiletic bulletin boards. And this is surely not wrong. Few texts of the New Testament could better serve as a motto on the minister's desk than the five-word phrase of the letter of James which even Luther honored highly: "Faith without works is dead." In comparison with sermons which, in trying to give meaning to the word "faith," interpret this as mere acceptance, on pain of excommunication, of a doctrinal system of belief, orthodox though this may be, the layman's revolt against what he labels "theology" and his preference for hortatory moralism is not surprising. But in yielding to this demand without a realization of its dread pitfalls, the preacher may be apostate to the Word of God. Proclaiming a message of reconciliation as a mere *ought* or *must* or ideal will not produce the reconciliation. Alienation of man from man has, as our existentialist analysis illustrated, deep roots. The cure involves nothing short of a drama of death and resurrection, a conversion and a new birth. And for this more is needed than ever so glowing picturizations of a utopia of human brotherhood and of the pathway to it a working out of our own salvation under our own power — even if we warn that this involves religious resources, help by way of prayer and fasting, and paying lip service to the First Commandment as well as to the Second.

I venture to illustrate this warning by way of a homiletic example. One of the passages of the New Testament most obviously applicable for a sermon on love of neighbor is the parable of the good Samaritan (Luke 10:29-37). When we come, in dealing with it in a step-by-step exposition, to the exhortation "Go and do likewise," our hearers are frequently left with the impression that here is precisely a call to moral heroism. Here is our familiar New Testament ethical idealism. "Our reach," to paraphrase Browning's familiar line, will, of course, "exceed our grasp," but that is what heaven is for.

If, however, our exposition of the parable is true to what it actually tells us, the final command to do likewise retains its place, but it is preceded by "theology." It digs deeply. For a full commentary on it we may have to turn to Paul's letter to the Romans. The parable begins with a question by a lawyer, obviously a pious Jew familiar with the law. He asks, "Who is my neighbor?" He wants the law, which he deeply reveres, defined. How else can law-religion — or, in modern terms, the religion of ideals — receive concrete meaning? The parable ends, however, with a second question, this one addressed to the lawyer, and through him, as it were, to all law-religion. The parable had brought onto the scene three characters — a priest, a Levite, and the Samaritan. "Which of these three," asks Jesus, "do you think, *proved* neighbor to the man who fell among the robbers?" (Italics mine.) The Samaritan had not asked, "Who is my neighbor?" He was simply a neighborly person, inwardly transformed so as to exemplify not law-obedience but sheer grace. To imitate the good Samaritan may require, accordingly, receiving a similar transformation. Can we achieve this ourselves? Or are we, as we listen to our Lord's parable, ushered into the thought world, as already suggested, of Paul? We are in the midst of the whole spectrum of New Testament theology. We confront the problem of law and grace, of justification by faith, of the imitation of Christ (the only perfect good Samaritan) by way of a baptismal dying with him and rising with him into the transformed life of a new creation in the fellowship of the Holy Spirit. The ministry of reconciliation, even as we deal with the concrete, mundane problems of men and women in the secular world, will involve all this.

In revealing to us the depth dimension of the problem of reconciliation between man and man, the Bible gives us little encouragement for trying to solve the problem by way of mere good advice or appeals to innate human power. Even such beloved concepts as discipleship of Jesus or imitation of Christ will need the underpinning of a theology that goes far beyond hortatory eloquence. Present them as ideals merely in their own right, extracted from their setting in the Biblical drama as a whole, and we may be preaching a salvation by works alone, a gospel ultimately of despair.

A worship of impersonal human ideals in place of the personal God of Biblical revelation has already received critical attention in the previous chapter's picture of humanism as a rival of Christianity. A further word of warning, however, against its allurements may be in order — particularly when such worship is presented in Christian camouflage, with texts from Holy Scripture freely at its beck and call. Almost the whole spectrum of Biblical concepts can, as it were, pass through a reminting process and appear as new coinage. The concept of the law is a crucial example. How tempting it is to present the demands of God as the Old Testament voices them as if they were ideals beckoning to performance and needing merely the proof of their social utility to give them motivating power. If, however, we realized the radical difference between an ideal and a commandment, we should at once be given pause. Ideals, or "values" (that favorite word in humanist ideology), are impersonal. They may, indeed, invite us to moral endeavor, and can serve as a mirror in which we see our ethical failures. Their lodgment in the human heart may be a token that God has not left himself without witness even in the religionless man. But how easily we can make our peace with an ideal! We can even create ideals and dream utopian dreams.

An encounter with a commandment, by way of contrast, even one uttered by a human custodian of power, is different in kind from a gentle dialogue with an ideal or a value. The dialogue now — above all when it is a dialogue between man and God — is between ourselves and One who has our personal destiny in his hands. Disobedience means nothing less than a verdict of death. " It is a fearful thing to fall into the hands of

the living God," says the author of the letter to the Hebrews
(ch. 10:31). No philosophy of ideals, not even that of a Socra-
tes or a Plato, has ever pictured an ideal as uttering a warning
like that! In an encounter with the God of the Bible, the farther
the dialogue proceeds, the more hopeless our state becomes.
We are on the way to making our own the cry of Paul's, " Who
will deliver me from this body of death? " (Rom. 7:24), or the
similar cry of the disciples, " Who then can be saved? " (Matt.
19:25).

We modern American Christians, lulled to ease of conscience
by the almost totalitarian reign of a humanist ideology in the
educational systems of the land from kindergarten to university, can scarcely conceive any longer what a realistic submission to the thought world of the Bible could involve. Phrases
such as " We were by nature children of wrath " or " dead
through . . . [our] trespasses and sins " (Eph. 2:3, 1), or
Paul's insistence on the necessity of salvation by grace and not
by works simply pass over our heads. " Does this actually mean,"
people ask, " that all our trying to be good does not count with
God? " We can soothe their concern — granted that they have
even come so far in their understanding of the Bible as to have
such a concern — to a certain degree, of course, but the scandal
of the Bible remains.

We could profit, clergy and laity alike, from seeing the hope-
lessness of meeting the living God of the Biblical revelation
with nothing but our easy worship of ideals in our hands,
as at least one of the writers of the Old Testament period
describes such an encounter. The passage is found in the Apoc-
rypha and echoes only one strain in the Old Testament law-religion, but it can serve as background for the hymns of surprised joy over the good news of the cross and the resurrection
which filled the air in the days of the early church. In a passage
of II Esdras (ch. 7:47-49, 53) we can listen, as it were, to a
final cry of despair over the failure of every human effort to
achieve reconciliation with God. It is as if Isaiah's " Woe is me!
For I am lost! " had become a universal cry, with no word of

comfort as yet on the horizon. I cite the passage from the Authorized Version, since it refuses to soften the author's confession of despair as do some later versions.

For what profit is it for men now in this present time to live in heaviness, and after death to look for punishment?
O thou Adam, what hast thou done? For though it was thou that sinned, thou art not fallen alone, but all that come of thee.
For what profit is it unto us, if there be promised us an immortal time, whereas we have done the works that bring death?
And that there should be shewed a paradise whose fruit endureth forever, wherein is security and medicine, since we shall not enter into it?

When we turn to the New Testament, keeping in mind the way in which many of the church's laity have somehow been led to read it, the fear of a God of inexorable law seems at first sight to have been left behind. If the strange language of Paul about law and grace could be deleted, the illusion of entering a world of " cheap grace," to use Bonhoeffer's by now familiar phrase, might receive some excuse. A biography of Jesus can, so it seems, be extracted from the record which ushers us into the presence of no figure more awesome than a teacher of ideals. A humanist philosopher like John Dewey has no difficulty in honoring the founder of Christianity as a kind of pre-scientific professor of ethics. To present Jesus to many of our contemporary devotees of " religion in general " as literally the commanding God of the Old Testament " in the flesh " comes as a shock. Even if that God of Moses and the prophets is still acknowledged as some kind of archaic deity in the background, has he not now, in the teachings of Jesus, become the benign Father whom we address familiarly as such even in the Lord's Prayer? As for the teachings of the Master — here, surely, the grim law-religion of Deuteronomy (ch. 28, for example) has been transmuted into the idealism of a utopian social dream, but all the more attractive for that very reason.

A reading of the Sermon on the Mount, accordingly, leaves the conscience of many modern Christians, for whom a humanist interpretation of religion has been their meat and drink, undisturbed. The appeal to love of neighbor, when it is interpreted as love even of an enemy, or when it asks for philanthropy to the point of giving a beggar our cloak as well as our coat, is, of course, a bit impractical. But we are accustomed to the impracticality of ideals. Realizing in action our democratic way of life is impractical also, but the discrepancy does not rob us of much peace of mind.

A gigantic task awaits the educational ministry of the churches in confronting the reigning humanist concept of our human predicament with the thought world of the Bible. The Sermon on the Mount could serve as a test case. Have those who boast of accepting it as a cluster of ideals which, though with lapses, can be actualized if men of goodwill only try hard enough, ever really read it? " Think not that I have come to abolish the law and the prophets; I have come not to abolish them but to fulfil them." (Matt. 5:17.) This law which is to be fulfilled is precisely the law of Deuteronomy — the same law that brought terror to the author of II Esdras and led Paul to confess despair in the presence of its ultimate demands. " The very commandment which promised life proved to be death to me." (Rom. 7:10.) The Sermon, as a friend of mine described its effect colloquially, plugs up the ratholes in the law of Moses so that even the morally perfect Pharisee fails to pass the test. As demand for law fulfillment it is a dress rehearsal of Judgment Day. A recent writer interprets the realistic meaning of the Sermon thus: " The Messiah, by his fulfillment of the law, both in his exposition of it in the Sermon on the Mount and in his embodiment of it in his death, has cast a lurid light upon the fact that all our *righteousnesses* are filthy rags. How awful is the judgment passed upon us by the Sermon on the Mount! " [43]

The Bible does not present the problem of reconciliation between man and man as one that can be solved short of a radical cure. A power beyond our own must come into play. Memory of Scripture passages that rob man of his self-trust can yield a rich harvest. "Cursed is the man who trusts in man and makes flesh his arm." "The heart is deceitful above all things, and desperately corrupt; who can understand it?" (Jer. 17:5, 9.) Turn to the opening chapters of the book of Genesis, and Jeremiah's verdict is verified in dread dramatic form. We misread the story of Cain and Abel if we do not see it as applicable to all of Adam's race. The story is one of fratricide — and this, too, before an altar in the midst of religious worship. We witness history's first murder in a cathedral, one that has had many a sequel.

If the sin of fratricide is limited to actual shedding of blood, pleading innocence and boasting that we are not like this human ancestor of ours may be easy. But if we listen to our Lord's reinterpretation of the command "You shall not kill," we find ourselves guilty despite all our boasting. We are guilty of murder even when we perform an act apparently so insignificant as calling a neighbor a fool or being angry with a brother (Matt. 5:21-22). Our murderous impulses within the heart may be held in check by fear of reprisal and by the necessity of a social compact leading to peace under the rule of law. But the reconciliation is on the surface only. Envy and jealousy and the rebellion against both our Creator and our neighbor whenever we feel ourselves cheated of talents or recognition is still there. We, in our turn, have suffered murder in the form of neglect or scorn and know that such an experience can be more painful than physical death. All this is vivid in experience even when we limit our insights to our relationships between man and man. Bring the holy God into the courtroom scene and all we can do is to cry, "Who will deliver me from this body of death?" (Rom. 7:24).

It can come as a shock to us to find that the chasm of alienation is not absent even in our Christian communal life. There are still murders in cathedrals. Dietrich Bonhoeffer urges ministers to be fully aware of this power of the evil one and to avoid illusory trust in churchly piety as they shepherd their congregations. I cite a vivid paragraph from his *Life Together:*

From the first moment when a man meets another person, he is looking for a strategic position he can assume and hold over against that person. There are strong persons and weak ones. If a man is not strong, he immediately claims the right of the weak as his own and uses it against the strong. There are gifted and ungifted persons, simple people and difficult people, devout and less devout, the sociable and the solitary. Does not the ungifted person have to take up a position just as well as the gifted person, the difficult one as well as the simple? And if I am not gifted, then perhaps I am devout anyhow; or if I am not devout, it is only because I do not want to be. May not the sociable individual carry the field before him and put the timid, solitary man to shame? Then may not the solitary person become the undying enemy and ultimate vanquisher of his social adversary? Where is there a person who does not with instinctive sureness find the spot where he can stand and defend himself, but which he will never give up to another, for which he will fight with all the drive of his instinct of self-assertion? All this can occur in the most polite or even pious environment.[44]

The ministry of reconciliation, when thus seen in its depth dimension, is truly a formidable calling. How can we fulfill its demands?

Clearly, we shall be compelled to recover, if we have ever lost it, a fresh appreciation of the church's ministry of the Word, be this by way of sermon or classroom lecture or simple dialogue on a street corner or a " gossiping of the gospel " at a dinner party. A pastoral ministry on its own, as it were, without the ministry of the Word as backdrop, is lost in the bogs of mere natural religion. And this ministry of the Word must be an unabashed theological word ministry. The layman's cry for mere practical religion, a term that he interprets as inspirational moralizing, must, on occasions at least, be ignored, or his understanding of what practical Christianity really means given a new interpretation. He may be right in his withdrawal from a sermon parading the conceptual abstractions of the theology of the schools. But the theology of the law and grace of the Bible is not initially one of conceptual abstractions. It is revelation in the form of event and act -- a majestic drama of salvation. If the word "practical" is accorded its root meaning of act or deed, is there anything more practical than the realistic experiences of our common life symbolized by such concepts as sin and forgiveness, guilt and judgment, trust and obedience? The word "reconciliation" may not be part of a layman's daily vocabulary, but what it describes a child can understand. By way of analogy, a school examination and a resultant passing or failing grade can unlock for a child even some of the most difficult doctrinal symbols of Biblical faith — Judgment Day, hell and heaven, the suffering of loneliness, and the joy of justification by grace.

In other words, the ministry of reconciliation, insofar as it has in view the realization in our common life of obedience to the Second Commandment of the law, requires concomitant obedience to the First Commandment. Every solution to the problem of how we can still live with one another, if attempted on the horizontal plane alone, will prove impossible. At the end, if not at the beginning, of the ministry of reconciliation between man and man, the vertical dimension looms on the horizon. Reconciliation is possible only as a triune relationship is established — God, the self, and the neighbor. We shrink, however, from a confrontation with the awesome presence of the Holy One. In a moral lawsuit, he robs even the one who, from a legal point of view, has right on his side of the privilege of self-righteous boasting. Even when the one thus in the right is moved to magnanimous excusing of the fault of his more guilty neighbor, and a remitting of the penalties, the solution is not in sight. We treat forgiveness all too often as a mere virtue that can receive human cultivation on its own. Paul's matchless chapter on charity is easily misunderstood. Perhaps it should never be read without being linked to the preceding chapter, which makes clear that Paul is not writing a treatise on social ethics but is describing the fruit of the Holy Spirit in the new life in the body of Christ. Kierkegaard's vivid epigram, "The opposite of sin is not virtue, but faith," could give pause to many a homiletic masterpiece on moral improvement.

It may seem ungracious to place question marks against the appeal for mutual forgiveness which the church's ministers are tempted to address to those who come for help in a story of shattered love or a broken relationship. Of course, mutual forgiveness is the result ultimately hoped for. But if mutual forgiveness is tried as between man and man alone, God not a party to the reconciling drama, the last state of that relationship may be worse than the first. Is there ever an action more open to self-righteousness than precisely one in which we have achieved the moral heroism of forgoing a legal right for retribution? Here is a weapon of pride that can be wielded time and again. Many a wife has ostensibly forgiven an erring husband, and may, indeed, have intended a true reconciling action, but can she readily surrender her consciousness of moral superiority? Can the forgiven party ever recover, in Bonhoeffer's phrase, "the spot where he can defend himself" as a person no longer in permanent stance of moral inferiority?

A concrete illustration may be of service here. A friend of mine, chaplain to students in one of our universities, relates the following incident. He had before him a student group with whom he had been discussing the doctrine of the atonement. He launched, by way of vivid analogy, on a retelling of the story of a broken and restored marriage relationship found in the opening chapters of The Book of Hosea. Gomer, the wife, had proved unfaithful to her marriage vow. Deserted, however, by her lovers for a day, she finds herself on a slave market. The husband, motivated by reconciling grace, buys back his faithless wife. The story is, clearly, as the prophet Hosea himself comes to see it, a drama-parable of the love of God for his sinning people — a drama of "redemption." My friend enjoyed the prospective thrill of having made an impression on his student group. He was brought to silence, however, when a girl in the group interrupted with the comment: " Ah, but how Gomer must have hated Hosea the rest of her life! " Such a conclusion is, alas, a possibility in a human reconciliation drama. What right had the magnanimous husband to bring

full consciousness of shame upon *her?* What may well have
been her subsequent reputation among her neighbors? Hosea's
reputation would have been safe enough. " What a wonderful
husband to take that worthless creature back into his home! "
But what of her? [45]

No — it is only when God's forgiveness has broken the pride
of both parties in a drama of reconciliation between man and
man that a true healing can appear on the scene. The one who
is asked to forgive the guilty must surrender the pride of self-
righteousness and see it as a sin more grievous than adultery
or murder or any mere law violation. The guilty party, in turn,
must surrender in repentance the equally deadly pride of self-
defense. They must each free the other to receive reconciliation
as a gift to both at once.

As we thus try to explore the mystery of the reconciling
gospel of the Bible, we may get a fresh understanding of why
Paul could choose as one of his major theme songs " justification by faith," or, to use the variant phrase, possibly less open
to misunderstanding, " justification by grace through faith "
(Eph. 2:8).

Now the righteousness of God has been manifested apart from law,
although the law and the prophets bear witness to it, the righteousness of God through faith in Jesus Christ for all who believe.
For there is no distinction; since all have sinned and fall short of
the glory of God, they are justified by his grace as a gift, through
the redemption which is in Christ Jesus. (Rom. 3:21-24.)

Puzzling language this, at first? Indeed, if left in a realm of
doctrinal abstractions, it can remain puzzling to all except
the learned doctors of the schools. But if translated into the
language of human relationship, it can leap to life. Paul is
touching upon the universal hunger of every man and every
woman in our fallen world — our need for recognition.[46]
Atheist and Christian can unite in seeing this as underlying our
human drama of man as he meets his neighbor. We fight for
our place in the sun, the spot where the lonely individual " can

stand and defend himself." And this involves the endless toil of self-justification — a task that can lead to moral heroism as well as the dread act of murder — often, if murder is seen in its true colors, to both at once. The moral Pharisee exhibits such toiling and its result in full paradox. Salvation, if self-justification is the goal sought, is "by works alone." The need for recognition is so overpowering that we seek it even in hell, although we recognize this hell as "other people." It is they who compel us, as we try to satisfy our hunger for recognition, to submit to the tyranny of conformity, to the sleepless care of keeping in repair the mask that others see.

But does all this toiling and this search for justification by works alone produce a heaven of charity and love? Can it even give birth to a true friendship? Can it exorcise envy and jealousy from the human heart, the seed-plot of the sin of Cain? A lover who has won the affection of a loved one — granted that the love drama looks toward the vows involved in what poets call "true love" — can be a witness to the futility of self-justification to secure his prize. He has had a glimpse of what justification by grace means. The miracle of love has happened by way of an undeserved gift. Alas, when the honeymoon gives way to endurance of the daily round, this token experience of justification by grace proves to be a frail foundation for permanent life together. As husband and wife they need the full gospel of reconciliation through grace, its power not limited to weak human idealism, but in Paul's phrase, "through the redemption which is in Christ Jesus."

Can we, accordingly, find manifestations of true reconciliation between man and man anywhere except in the body of Christ, the church? Its manifestations are imperfect there also — tokens only of life in the Kingdom. The Christian, too, is always still a sinner, justified only by grace through faith. But the dynamism of the Holy Spirit does work miracles of reconciliation, as forgiven prodigal sons meet to glorify the Father's love and discover in that worship a bond of union with one another. Any pastor can share with his brethren testimonies of joyous reconciliation which make glad even the angels in heaven.

An earlier chapter has pleaded the cause of secular or worldly evangelism — the good news of the incarnation carried out into a religionless world. Such evangelism leaves the safety of the sanctuary and, like the incarnate Lord it serves, is willing to "eat with publicans and sinners" (Mark 2:16). But this evangelism must come full circle. Christ wants to be host at a feast as well as gracious guest in yet alien households. His disciples are commissioned as his servants to go into the highways and to bid to his marriage banquet as many as they shall find (Matt. 22:9) — "the poor, the maimed, the lame, the blind" (Luke 14:13). This ministry of welcome may turn out to be as great a test of faithful evangelism as is the call to "go into all the world."

French evangelistic literature has brought to the fore three words that summarize by way of three successive steps the church's mission strategy. The three words are: *présence, service, communication* (give them the honor of French pronunciation, and they escape the handicap of shopworn familiarity). Incarnational evangelism is first of all the *présence* of the church in the world. Though not much has been said in this exposition of *service* (*diakonia*, or "deaconing"), presence and service are intimately related. Communication, however, must wait until its hour has come. Witness to the gospel must win the right to be heard. When, however, it has won that right, the church as "Christ in community" can alone finally give to those prepared for a meeting with the church's Lord, the foretaste of the Kingdom of Heaven which is the gospel's climax and glory.

Is the church of our day fulfilling its vocation of communicating the reconciling grace of the gospel to our world? The next chapter will try to highlight this question.

Chapter IV

The Witness of the Gathered People of God

That the church is in some sense involved in communicating the gospel to those outside its life is probably admitted by all who call themselves Christians. Every church member today knows that his local congregation has an obligation to something called " evangelism " and to something called " missions." The call to evangelism causes little disturbance. The word is commonly understood as belonging to the promotional vocabulary of a church as institution. The solicitation of new church members is accepted as an obligation resting on Christians almost as a matter of course. Growth in church membership and in financial support is essential for the life of every congregation. The call to evangelism does become disturbing, however, when the basic meaning of the word is unveiled. Evangelism is literally " gospeling," a proclamation of good news. To limit its meaning to the promotion of an institution, however ultimately worthy, is a tragic impoverishment. The good news of the incarnation and of the cross — we can recall John 3:16 — has no price tag attached to it, not even that of joining a church. Much of our popular understanding of evangelism stands under judgment.

A sad erosion of meaning has overtaken the word " missions " also. Even loyal churchmen are tempted to think of it, in its turn, as another promotional activity, but, unlike evangelism, promotion at a distance, and therefore a call on a church's resources only when these can boast of a surplus or overflow.

Although both evangelism and missions suffer from misunderstandings of their true meaning under the gospel, an analysis of this handicap as it applies to the concept of missions may deserve priority. Evangelism, as a matter of fact, is frequently subsumed under this more embracing symbol. We know it then as "home missions" as distinguished from "foreign missions."

Before attempting such an analysis, however, a clarification may be useful of the meaning of "church" as well as of the concept "missions." Both are in flux in our time. M. A. C. Warren, one of the most trusted missionary statesmen of today, imparts wise counsel when he warns that "both church and missions are much less familiar than we commonly think. Indeed, if we frankly admitted that we do in fact know very little about either of them, if we took them a little less for granted, we might begin to make the kind of discoveries that would change the world." [47]

To insert here an excursus on the doctrine of the church is, to be sure, impossible. One insight into the nature of the church, however, especially as this relates to evangelism and missions, may be helpful. I have made use of it in the titles of this and the following chapter. The Department on the Laity of the World Council of Churches has made current in ecumenical discourse the symbols "the gathered church" and "the scattered church." Both find their source in the analogy enshrined in the word addressed by Jesus to the disciples: "You are the salt of the earth" (Matt. 5:13). Salt, a precious substance in early times, is useless until it has been gathered, from mine or seawater, and purified. But it fulfills its function only if, after having been gathered, it is scattered to be again dissolved. Applied to the church, the salt symbol does permit, with reservations, a look at the problem of evangelism and missions with two manifestations of the church in mind. The first — it will be the theme of this chapter — views the church principally as an assembled group. The symbol of scattered salt then will lend itself to a look at the people of God at work in the world.

That a strange gulf exists in popular understanding between church and missions admits of little doubt. There are historical reasons for this gulf. The great missionary societies that have carried the gospel to Asia and Africa and the western islands grew up as separate organizations from the churches as churches. They drew their support from church people and still do, but " missions " appealed to loyalties not quite identical with those evoked by " church." Even the ecumenical movement has been nurtured in our century in two separate streams of unifying structures — the World Council of Churches on the one hand and the International Missionary Council on the other. The two structures have now become organizationally united.[48] But it may require generations to heal the chasm between church and mission in conceptual understanding and even more in practice. " The separation of these two things," writes Bishop Lesslie Newbigin, " which God has joined together, must be adjudged one of the great calamities of missionary history, and the healing of this division one of the great tasks of our time." [49]

The task is, indeed, not an easy one. It may require the combined efforts of theologians, missionary statesmen, and a new Pentecostal invasion of the Holy Spirit to accomplish what is needed. A call looking toward a radical rethinking of " The Life and Mission of the Church," [50] issued by the World Student Christian Federation, defines the new vision of the church which a reunion of church and mission will demand as deserving the name of a Copernican revolution.

To sketch this Copernican revolution even in outline, however, is a hazardous undertaking, and I am under no illusions that the profound mysteries of both church and missions will here be unveiled. Yet even a trial journey of exploration may be worthwhile.

That the church *has* a missionary vocation, as already suggested, is probably nowhere denied by any Christian congregation. The missionary budgets of the churches of Europe and America still mount up to millions of dollars, marks, and pounds. It is only when advocates of a Copernican revolution introduce the slogan "The church *is* mission" — the word "mission" now appearing in the singular as distinguished from "missions" in the plural — only then are we brought up with a start.

The layman in the pew is still familiar with John 3:16, with its glowing assertion that "God so loved the world" as to send his Son for that whole world's redemption. He joins in the singing of the Agnus Dei, with its cry for mercy to One who takes away "the sins of the world." He listens to Christ's command to his disciples, as recorded in the closing verses of Matthew's Gospel, to "go . . . and make disciples of all nations," or the parallel commission recalled by John, "As the Father has sent me, even so I send you" (John 20:21), or the equally clear directive to the apostles before his ascension, "You shall be my witnesses in Jerusalem and in all Judea and Samaria and to the end of the earth" (Acts 1:8). That there are men and women who listen to this call for a continuing witnessing vocation today as did the disciples in their time is a familiar fact also. Missionaries and evangelists appear in pulpits and in revival meetings voicing the call for missionary support. But the vocation, in this missionary outreach, of the church as "church," especially as it exists in the form of a localized congregation? This, as popularly understood, has the function of being the receptacle into which those converted by an evangelist or missionary can be welcomed. It is not itself the missionary agency.

Multiplication of such receptacles is desirable, of course, offering a variety of spiritual harbors so as to give the convert the choice of a fellowship congenial to his tastes. Once established, however, such a receptacle exists for the sake of its own members. The ministry exists for the purpose of serving the now established institution. The congregation is tempted to

congratulate itself for having built a peaceful spiritual haven
for its religious needs, walled off from the turmoil of the workaday world. A distinction exists, so we assume, between sacred
and secular concerns. The church nurtures those concerns
which we can identify as sacred — our prayer life, our hunger
for peace of mind, our need for fellowship.

It is not too difficult to see how our World Student Christian
Federation revolutionaries can indict many a church when it
has become a kind of cultural ghetto, safe behind protecting
walls, as in need of a Copernican revolution. I, too, shall join
in such an indictment. Yet the indictment needs the check of
charity and understanding. Something is right as well as wrong
in this manifestation of the gathered people of God withdrawn
from the world. The word "refuge" as well as the word "mission" is found in our Bible and our hymns as descriptive of
temple and sanctuary. The fellowship of the Holy Spirit must
discover itself as a corporate body of Christ before it can un-
dertake a mission to those still outside. An army has to be
taught how to halt as well as how to march. "Gather the people to me, that I may let them hear my words" (Deut. 4:10),
says God to Moses in the days when the church of the Old
Covenant first emerges from its slavery under alien rule.
Groups of Christians have appeared again and again in Christian history, taking seriously the counsel of Paul: "Come out
from them, and be separate from them, says the Lord, and
touch nothing unclean; then I will welcome you, and I will be
a father to you, and you shall be my sons and daughters, says
the Lord Almighty" (II Cor. 6:17-18). Such sectarian groups
present a problem to ecumenical movements, but who can
deny that they have exercised a strange power of gospel witness?

Nevertheless, the call for a Copernican revolution in our
understanding of the relation between church and mission deserves a full hearing. Our recent literature of evangelism
abounds in indictments verging on bitter satire, of the self-
worshiping church, the introverted church, the secularized

church, the church whose god resembles at times a local Baal, watching over a local sanctuary only, one safely protected behind closed doors. A recent sociological study of the typical church on the American scene uses the phrase " the organization church " to describe it as it manifests itself, in prosperous suburbia at least. Organization is contrasted with organism. A congregation can flourish as an organization marvel and yet fail as an organic manifestation of " Christ as community." [51]

Self-preservation of the church as an institution receives unquestioned priority — more and more comfortable pews and more and more comfortable kneeling cushions, to play with a bit of satire, for less and less painful prayers of repentance. It may shock us to be told that many a congregation of our time is, in the Biblical view, guilty of idolatry. Its god is no longer the Lord of the whole earth and of all nations. The author of the last book of the Bible may have had such idolatry in mind as he places the church of Laodicea under judgment: " For you say, I am rich, I have prospered, and I need nothing; not knowing that you are wretched, pitiable, blind, and naked " (Rev. 3:17).

It is easy to exaggerate such criticism of our church life in America and Europe, the missionary homelands of the gospel. There are always, as Elijah discovered as he yielded to a mood of discouragement, " seven thousand in Israel, all the knees that have not bowed to Baal " (I Kings 19:18). Yet prophetic warnings are clearly in order. I venture to picture this dark side of our self-worshiping church life by way of an analogy or parable. I borrow this from an essay on evangelism of my own now safely entombed in a dated journal on library shelves:

Picture a coast guard or lifesaving station on a dangerous coast. It has stood for centuries, and tales of its rescue service are treasured by the successors of the founders. In the course of time, those who manned the rescue service turned to beautifying the station itself. Do not lifesavers deserve comfort and a rest home to fit them for their arduous task? Architects vied with one another in building for them a station worthy of the cause they served. Honorary, though not active, members of the company of rescuers joined in lending support. The station-building, however, became in time such an absorbing activity that rescue service itself was increasingly neglected, although rescue drills and rituals were carefully preserved. The actual launching out into ocean storms became a hireling vocation or one left to a few volunteers. What was even more a deflection of the original charter of the station, when the dedicated volunteers brought in their boatloads of the shipwrecked — men of alien color and speech, often maimed and encrusted with ocean slime — the custodians of the rescue station were often disconcerted. " Will they not," so they were tempted to exclaim, " soil the linen on our clean beds, and, moved by gratitude of their rescue, desire to become lifesavers themselves and thus presume to belong by right to our intimate fellowship? Should we not set up a minimum entrance requirement of cleanliness and good manners before we offer shelter? We can, at least, urge them to build a lifesaving station of their own at a decorous distance from ours." [52]

Exaggerated satire? Yes, of course. But it can find parallels in many a sober confession on the part of pastors of actual congregations who pause in their race from one appointment to another for a look at their ministerial slavery. Here is one such confession, " hot off the griddle," reported in a recent book by one who served as executive secretary of the Department of Evangelism of the National Council of the Churches of Christ in the U.S.A. Paul Musselman cites from a letter of a minister of a prosperous suburban parish:

This is no longer a Christian fellowship. These are members of a Christian church who pay, and pay mighty well, to be serviced spiritually. In a way, I am not much better off, in some ways worse off, than the gas station attendant. They pay him to keep their cars in running condition. They pay me somehow to do something that will keep their lives from blowing into bits.[53]

The author who cites this devastating confession adds his own appraisal of the churches in American suburbia:

My own impression, after seven years of traveling throughout the country, is that the average minister is the handyman of our times.

He is expected to be some sort of a spiritual baby-sitter and to be proficient in the art of pandering to the immature preferences of the average, spiritually illiterate American.[54]

These outbursts of near-despair concerning the shape of religion in our supposedly flourishing Christianity of suburbia touch upon the burden placed on the ministry as it confronts the task of church renewal. They underscore, perhaps more vividly than is fair and yet with unmistakable cogency, the fact that a tragic gulf exists between church and mission on the part of many congregations' understanding of the gospel. The church can become an idol, and the ministry an idolatrous priesthood. Church and ministry are then thought to exist on behalf of the worshiping devotees of a god who is to be at our beck and call, answering our needs, pandering to our undisciplined desires, and keeping our American way of life intact and safe from harm.

It is not an accident, accordingly, that prophetic voices of our time, concerned with healing the break between church and mission, call first of all for a renewal of the church itself. For if a church that lives to itself, institutional self-preservation its primary goal, has exchanged worship of the true God for an idol of its own making, the opposite danger exists also. Mission without church is equally disastrous, though it may be admitted that defining the relation betwen the two is one of the major theological problems of our time. Is not the emergence of the church the climactic, mighty act of God which is of the very substance of the gospel itself? And is not the invitation to incorporation into this body of Christ the climactic appeal of gospel preaching? The mission command of our Lord in Matthew's Gospel bids the disciples not merely to teach all nations but to baptize them in the name of the Father, and of the Son, and — again climactically — in the name of the Holy Ghost, the latter Christ's continuing presence in his church. *Extra ecclesiam nulla salus* is still an ecumenically accepted dogma, however puzzling may be its theological implications.

Two apparently opposed views on the relation between church and mission are under debate in our time. Emil Brunner can say: " The ecclesia, the Christian society, belongs to the substance of the revelation and constitutes the true end of the latter. . . . Consequently, it is impossible to consider communion with the ecclesia as a means to an end; it must be realized that it is the end itself." [55] At the other extreme of conviction is the warning voiced by one of the most influential theologians of missions and evangelism of our time, J. C. Hoekendijk, of Holland: " Church-centric missionary thinking is bound to go astray, because it revolves around an illegitimate center." The author pleads for replacing the church, as the center and goal for evangelism and missions, by the eschatological Kingdom and the apostolate, the church not its own end but servant of the gospel's outreach to the whole world (the *oikoumenē*). " The planting of the church cannot be an adequate definition of the goal of missionary work; beyond the churches the mission is directed to the ends of the earth and the end of time." [56] In a word, to the problem of defining the right relationship between church and mission there must be added the exploration of their relationship to a third reality, the Kingdom of God itself, when both the church militant on earth and the mission will have performed their tasks and all things will be handed over to the Father.

I shall not venture on a premature resolution of this tension in the area of the theology of mission. We are only at the beginning of seeing light in our gropings for a full clarity of vision. Yet some insights may be on the horizon. I shall myself risk a brief presentation of three tentatively formulated clues to a clarification of the role of the church — the " gathered people of God " now chiefly in mind — as witnessing agent of the gospel.

The first suggests a rectification of an epithet applied to the church in an earlier paragraph, namely, that of being merely the receptacle into which converts of evangelizing endeavor were placed for further nurture and, as some might say,

for further exploitation. If a church limits its witnessing vocation to being a mere receptacle, judgment may be pronounced
upon it. But if the adjective "mere" is removed, judgment can
halt. The church as a welcoming community does have a vital
function to perform in the spread of the gospel.

A second function of the church in Christ's mission to the
world is that of serving as training ground and home base for
those who are to be the mission's shock troops sent into foreign territory. Without the church in Antioch, home base for
Paul, there might never have been a church of Corinth or of
Ephesus or of Philippi. This function of the church as training
station will receive special attention in the following chapter.

A third clue to the true relationship between church and mission, though it is the one most difficult to guard against misunderstanding, is the fact, rightly brought to the fore by Emil
Brunner, that the church is itself of the very substance of the
good news of the drama of salvation. And for *this* good news,
verbal proclamation and evangelistic preaching — yes, even the
outgoing "incarnational evangelism" hailed in my opening
chapter — are not enough. This must receive demonstration by
way of a community witnessing to what "church" means here
and now. Whole pages could be filled with descriptions of this
mystery — the continuing life of Christ in history. Here is a the-
ophany that, in the words of Paul, does not limit itself to "enticing words," but is a "demonstration of the Spirit and power"
(I Cor. 2:4). Can a message of reconciliation be really com-
municated except by a reconciled community?

As we look at this witnessing vocation of the gathered people of God, one of the most important symbols for the church
in the New Testament, which has already received repeated
allusion, forces itself on our attention. The church is the fellowship of the Holy Spirit. Even the original Greek word for
fellowship — *koinōnia* — is increasingly familiar, and may soon,
like the words *kērygma*, and *agapē*, and *diakonia*, become
common coin in the vocabulary of the instructed layman.
(Why should the laity be deprived of at least some contact

with the language in which the gospel has come to us?) What can the image of the church as *koinōnia Spiritu Sancti* mean to us?

Full theological enlightenment on the doctrine of the Holy Spirit may have to be a task assigned to the doctors of the schools. "The Holy Ghost," so Emil Brunner confesses, "has always been more or less the stepchild of theology and the dynamism of the Spirit a bugbear for theologians. . . . Theology, through its unconscious intellectualism, has often proved a significant restrictive influence, stifling the operations of the Holy Ghost, or at least their full creative manifestation." [57] The rediscovery of the witnessing power of Christian fellowship in action in parish and community, however, need not wait until full doctrinal enlightenment arrives. A conceptual understanding of the mystery of our common life in the body of Christ may well be a derivative of seeing it in action first. A descriptive analysis of Christian fellowship, accordingly, even if it consists of only a very modest exploratory voyage, may throw some light on this mystery.

Some form of life in community is a necessity for human existence — even, so a previous chapter has argued, in hell. Christianity has no monopoly of the experience of fellowship, or, to use the colloquial term of our day, of "togetherness." God has given to man from the outset of creation the gift of neighbors and the gift of the law which sustains the fabric of society. It is only in community that we discover ourselves as persons in the first place. Our existentialist philosophers have brought this insight into such prominence that it is not likely to be soon forgotten. Some of us may be wearied by now of the uncritical Kierkegaard worshiper or the "I-Thou" theme song of Martin Buber's, or have grown faint in trying to master the thought of the philosopher Heidegger. But, as more than one theologian testifies, we may have barely begun to adjust our theological world view, inherited from the era of rational scholasticism, to the depth dimension yawning before us as we explore the dynamism of personal life, of the "I" in encounter with a "Thou," and of the problem of communication between these islands of isolation.

Every human being is a mysterious "I," subject, not object. Yet he does not discover himself as a subject except in an encounter with other similar centers of consciousness. The person, as a self-conscious "I," is born only in community, in fellowship. I have met no more convincing exposition of this fundamental fact of human existence than a passage in one of Paul Tillich's writings, summarizing much existentialist insight.

No personal being exists without communal being. The person as the fully developed, individual self is impossible without other developed selves. If he did not meet the resistance of other selves, every self would try to make himself absolute. But the resistance of the other selves is unconditional. One individual can conquer the entire world of objects, but he cannot conquer another person without destroying him as a person. The individual discovers himself through this resistance. If he does not want to destroy the other person, he must enter into communion with him. In the resistance of the other person, the person is born. Therefore, there is no person without encounter with other persons. Persons can grow only in the communion of personal encounter.[58]

The social sciences of our day are increasingly aware of this basic need of human existence. A notable company of social scientists is engaged in a new field of research in human relations as this involves life in fellowships or groups. It is best known under the titles "group dynamics" or "human relations research." Under the sponsorship of the National Education Association, the results of this research are penetrating the educational scene of America at all levels. The business world has discovered it, as have civic and community leaders and the Armed Forces.

The history of the movement can be briefly summarized. Under the inspiration of Kurt Lewin, a social scientist of note who came to this country from Germany during the Hitler era, a research center in group dynamics was founded in the

1940's at the Massachusetts Institute of Technology. It has since moved to the University of Michigan, and its staff is serving as consultants in the solution of community problems all over the land. To implement genuine research in this new science — the study of group life — a Laboratory in Group Development was established at Bethel, Maine, where, during the summer months, those interested in the movement have subjected themselves to research disciplines.

During the summer of 1949, I was a lone clergyman at this laboratory among one hundred and fifty representatives of secular callings. In succeeding years the number of clergy attending the laboratory has rapidly multiplied. Some churches (the Protestant Episcopal Church in the U.S.A. a pioneer) have, indeed, found the insights gained by church leaders who have exposed themselves to group dynamics disciplines so important that they have incorporated into their adult education programs group life laboratories of their own. Since, however, contact with this new science of group dynamics is as yet only sporadic, but judged by those who have participated in its outreach, of unquestioned value for an understanding of what the revival of Christian fellowship can mean for the churches, a somewhat full description of a laboratory experience (I draw heavily on my own) will here be ventured.

The laboratory membership was, first of all, divided into small groups, averaging eighteen in number. Trainers were assigned to each group, but their role was largely one of silence, broken only by occasional warnings and general service as consultants. The group was on its own. Seated around an oval table for hours each day for three weeks, the group was given no agenda except the single directive: "Become a group!" This "becoming" began with chaos. All of us were accustomed to working in groups. But when had we ever been plunged into a group that did not have a task to give it meaning? Here we were on an open sea with no port on the horizon. Never before had we become aware of the way in which, in most of our past group experience, concentration on "doing" had isolated us from one another as persons. In the usual group, we use busyness and the pressure of time as excuses for disregarding the feelings of others or for brushing aside their opinions.

Here, however, with no agenda behind which to hide, our behavior stood out in stark relief. Egotistical speechmaking alternated with equally egotistical withdrawal. Tempers rose. A Napoleon or two attempted to take over. But all this floundering resulted in the gradual emergence of a corporate "body" with an *esprit de corps*, competent to tame its Napoleons, heal inferiority feelings, give status and vocation to the less gifted, and win every member to a surrender, partially at least, of his egocentricity to an overarching mystical corporateness. Few of those attending would refuse to describe the experience as a minor, undreamed of, miracle.

Alongside this more intimate discipline, the laboratory introduced us, in classroom sessions, to the growing body of research into group behavior, all pointing toward the stimulation, in our democratic community life, of participation and personal involvement. Detailed descriptions of all these findings would lead this essay too far afield: I limit myself to describing one that has already proved itself to be extraordinarily useful in many of our churches. Study of groups has made it clear that a fundamental aspect of any satisfying group experience is participation by every member. Yet think of the many group gatherings within the corporate life of our churches in which the majority of those present are expected to be mere passive observers. A simple method of involvement, now in common use, is the division of a gathering into small groups of five or six, to discuss a topic or to devise a question to be addressed to a speaker. In a brief time everyone, even in a large gathering, will have had the opportunity to say something, to be listened to, and to feel a part of what is taking place. Genuinely aroused interest is the almost inevitable result.

"The sons of this world are wiser in their own generation

than the sons of light." This verse of the New Testament must occur to many of those who, like myself, have enjoyed the privilege of intimate contact with the findings of group dynamics. Here are social scientists devoting themselves to the cause of a better community life in our secular democracy and to better educational methods in our schools, who are disclosing to the leadership in the churches opportunities and insights which the church has always had in its possession, but which often have lain fallow and unused. It was for me, a representative of the church's own ministry, something of a humiliating experience, during my stay at the Group Development Laboratory, to hear repeated many times: " This was the greatest religious experience of my life." Clearly, those who said this had failed to find in their church contacts the satisfactions which the church, when true to its nature, should have offered them in abundance and which can meet human needs far more basic than any for which even the best secular movements can provide a cure.

We are living in an age when the necessity of community, of membership in a group, of a life of fellowship and of belonging, is being rediscovered as a fundamental need of men and women. We are tired of being individualists — in our secular activities, first of all, but also in religion. We are opening our eyes to the fact that a person is something more than an isolated individual, or merely a human atom, lost in a collective. If it should be true that the contemporary church has also fostered fellowship-starved individualism or merely membership in an impersonal collective, though this devotes itself to pious exercises, the problem of reviving community ought to be for the church a major concern.

The word " group " is, of course, ambiguous. It can describe anything from a mob to what the New Testament has in mind when it speaks of two or three gathering together in a fellowship of common loyalty to a transcendent deity. A criticism might be directed to some of our social scientists for their naïve assumption that in the group experiences normal in our

American democracy fundamental loyalties to ethical ends can still be sufficiently taken for granted so that basic questions as to whether a group serves God or devil need not be raised. But before entering upon criticism, a prior question may have occurred to the reader — a question tentatively touched on in an earlier paragraph but not there given due weight. "Why should the church turn to a secular movement for help in understanding itself as life in community? Should not the direction of search have been reversed — secular leadership turning to the church as model and guide? Is not the church, as already indicated in an earlier paragraph, precisely a fellowship — the fellowship of the Holy Spirit, no less? And has not the church practiced life in fellowship for two thousand years so that it, not secular scientists, can lay claim to expert knowledge?"

In principle, this is no doubt true. Western secularism still lives on its Christian capital. The average group experience of Americans, to name no others, can still take respect of person and a minimum at least of fraternal concern for granted. The church has been the seed-plot of our community spirit and of our democratic communal traditions. But the rise in recent generations of purely secular fellowships, no longer conscious of their debt to the churches, and yet apparently satisfying needs that the churches do not meet, may indicate that the church has surrendered some at least of its rights and lost some at least of its powers. Secular fellowships have become rival " churches." They may be used of God to call the churches to judgment.

Anyone familiar with the current literature of self-examination on our religious bookshelves can testify that on few issues is the conscience of the churches more stirred than on that of the loss of the note of true fellowship, of a common life in the body of Christ, of social witness, and social unity. Individualist pietism has seemingly replaced brotherliness in both Roman Catholic and Protestant church life, and voices of prophecy are being heard in both traditions, calling us to repentance.

The liturgical movements active throughout Christendom all have as one of their aims the revival of lay participation in worship and the breaking down of walls between isolated ministry and isolated people. But the revolt against our atomized community life in the churches goes even deeper. We turn to the picture of Christian fellowship in the New Testament and are compelled to confess that our institutionalized churches (again both Roman Catholic and Protestant) offer little that resembles such group experience and lay participation. "When you come together," so Paul describes one of these meetings of Christians, "each one of you has a hymn, a lesson, a revelation, a tongue, or an interpretation. . . . Earnestly desire to prophesy, and do not forbid speaking in tongues." (I Cor. 14:26, 39.) When have we seen anything like this? Each one sharing with his fellow Christians a hymn or a lesson? "Each one" has nothing of the sort. We rarely participate in a church meeting except in the singing of a hymn or in an occasional chorus prayer.

When it comes to social witness as a unified people of God to secular life outside our formal worship services, we are in even worse plight. In an urban environment we hardly know one another except as anonymous sharers in a formalized worship act. The very word "parish" (*paroikia*, or neighborhood) frequently has little meaning. Our next-door neighbor worships, let us say, in the Methodist church a mile north, while we attend the Episcopal church two miles south. We meet our neighbors on the level of gossip, or of talk on the weather, or of quarreling about property rights, but we do not bring these concerns of neighborliness into a common meeting before God where we can submit them to judgment. Even as members of a single denomination we frequently choose our place of worship not on a basis of geographical parish boundaries, but because of individualist liturgical preference or because "we like the Reverend Mr. Blank." Ours are coterie churches. At times they are mere religious "clubs." Proof of the latter indictment could consist in the fact that we are often tempted to place social requirements for church membership above repentance and Baptism.

The picture of the contemporary church need not be all black, of course. Many tokens of revival of communal Christian life can be cited to balance a critical view. My objective at the moment is merely to plead for willingness on the part of church leaders to submit to lessons we can learn from our secular friends. If group experience of some kind is an essential note of life in the church, all insight into the nature of that experience ought to be welcomed. Pastoral counseling with individuals is profiting greatly from the wisdom contributed by psychiatric science and depth psychology. We do not need to become Freudians to learn something from Sigmund Freud. The study of group life can give experimental proof of the literally enormous effect upon personal maturing of such experiences, only to be found in life in community, as participation, acceptance, the enduring of rejection, respect for minority opinion, submission to corporate discipline and to objective evaluation of our individual character traits, discovery of hitherto unused or even unsuspected socially useful talents, and many more. Transfer the scene from secular or religiously neutral group life to that of " church," and the possibility of a parallel ministry leaps to the eye.

When Paul — to refer again to his Corinthian letter and its vivid description of an early Christian parish meeting — lays down rules of procedure, he is writing a manual of group dynamics! For example: " Let two or three prophets speak, and let the others weigh what is said. If a revelation is made to another sitting by, let the first be silent." (I Cor. 14:29-30.) A church meeting in Corinth evidently wrestled with a problem that has confronted every assembly in which free speech is permitted from that day to this: What does a chairman do with the " regular speakers " who monopolize the discussion? The fourth chapter of Paul's Ephesian letter, in turn, gives a priceless picture of Christian community life on a level of brotherliness and mutual sharing of burdens which could make a secular social scientist gasp. " Let all bitterness and wrath and anger and clamor and slander be put away from you, with all malice, and be kind to one another, tenderhearted, forgiving one another, as God in Christ forgave you." (Eph. 4:31-32.)

The church, accordingly, can lay claim to powers for creating a communal life of charity which are not found outside its borders. Our social scientists do not write monographs on the doctrine of the Holy Spirit. Nor do they refer man to divine grace for a solution of his interpersonal problems. They may speak of acceptance, but not of forgiveness; of unsocial behavior, but not of sin against God. Yet, granted that the uniqueness of the church, when true to its nature, as over against any comparable social phenomenon must be kept in mind, analogies between the church and group life outside the church can prove helpful. Analogy has an honorable place in the history of theology. Jesus employed the method of parables boldly. " The kingdom of heaven is like . . ." and then follow pictorially vivid scenes of ordinary Palestinian culture, at times ethically shocking.

Few words have received heavier underscoring in scientific study of group experience than the word " participation." The value of participation in any social endeavor may seem obvious. Yet its importance in promoting personal maturing needs to be experienced in laboratory testing to be fully appreciated. It is truly amazing in how few decisions that are asked of us we are participants in the authority that does the asking. Parents, teachers, the office " boss," the factory system, even the church with its ministry — all exercise authority over us. We are free to obey or to rebel, no doubt, but how seldom are we participants in formulating the content, or the *what*, of the decision to which we are to give consent or refusal. Our value as servants of a cause or institution may receive exaltation. We may, in the commercial community, be paid high wages (even slaves at times brought a high price in the slave market). But we are often mere impersonal pawns on an authoritarian chessboard. Real life, however, should be personal, not impersonal, en-

counter. Hence, when authoritarianism is surrendered and
participation in formulating the decisions to which we are to
give consent is invited, a minor miracle happens. The "person" is born. Our opinion counts as well as our vote or our
loyalty. Status and human dignity are gifts of participation.

Are there dangers in authoritarian surrender? Yes, of course.
Participation soon runs into the necessity of limits and boundaries to freedom. Social chaos is a possibility. All human life is
under authority — the authority of natural and revealed law,
as also of the wisdom of science and of tradition. But authority
needs to be distinguished from authoritarianism. In the church,
obviously, no democracy, even of saints, can replace the authority of God, or of the gospel, or of a duly instituted ministry.
But there are large areas of freedom left in which even the
humblest layman could exercise his gifts. Surely a Women's
Guild in a parish might be given the privilege of participation
in the life of God's people beyond deciding whether ham or
chicken is to be on the menu of the next parish supper!

Laboratory testing of group experience which boldly tries
permissive freedom can prove that dangers are easily exaggerated. A group consciously permissive may discover that
what are known as "Quaker" or unanimous decisions are a
normal result. It is easy, for example, for the majority in a
group to achieve a triumph for its opinion by a rapidly secured
majority vote. To accord minority opinion full voice, involving
at times long and painful listening to folly or even hostility,
looks like a waste of time. It may even endanger the prevailing
of right. But let a group try permissive methods and it may receive a surprise.

Men and women hunger for status and acknowledgment of
their worth as individuals more than for victory of an opinion.
They may champion a wrong or partial view precisely for the
sake of receiving notice as persons in place of being mere vot-
ing fodder in a collective. If they discover that they *are* given
dignity as persons, are listened to, are accorded the privilege
of belonging, despite their hostility, gratitude for this grace

may soon replace the hostility and the stubborn prejudice. Listening to reason — the matured reason of the majority, let us assume — is no longer an indignity.

Participation, as a matter of fact, is only one of many concepts whose significance careful observation of group experience can underscore. Related to it, and in part corollaries or parallels, are those of "acceptance" and "rejection." We do not, of course, need a gospel of group dynamics to inform us of their importance. We may be tempted, in fact, in religious discourse, to substitute for them at once the more hallowed concepts of forgiveness and judgment, of grace and law, of mercy and wrath. Yet here again scientific study of group behavior can bring rich insights. Our Biblical vocabulary has become shopworn. It may receive new meaning by way of analogies found in secular experience.

One insight that a laboratory group experience implants deeply in the consciousness of an observer deserves special mention. This is the realization, often striking the observer by surprise, of the enormous *power* latent in a group, provided that it has achieved maturity and unity of purpose.

The total community of nation or tribe has powers over its members of life or death. Every fractional community shares in these powers. Acceptance or rejection, as already suggested, can be equated with life or death in the realm of personal relationships. Every group in which acceptance touches depth of personality has powers of healing personality neuroses. The timid can be given courage. The shy and tongue-tied can receive the gift of speech (one thinks of the "gift of tongues" widespread in the church of New Testament times). Buried talents can be brought out into the open and made socially useful. Even confessed ignorance can induce the learned members of a group to develop pedagogic sharing of their educational privileges.

This group dynamism, it must be pointed out, is not a monopoly of "good" groups. Community life under the domination of evil or neutral spirits possesses this power also. The

Nazi youth movement had it, as do the communist cells flourishing around the world today. A labor union " local," in which participation in decision-making thrives, transforms a factory " hand " into a person. It consequently wins a loyalty denied to an impersonal industrial corporation, even if the latter should offer as bribes to loyalty benefits far exceeding those which the labor union can provide.

If our attention now turns to the church, we are aware that it clearly faces rivals in its appeal for the souls of men. It has no monopoly of " spiritual " power. Every group solidarity has at work within it an *esprit de corps*, an empowering corporate spirit. It is this which molds the members into the pattern set by the community. It is this which imparts strength to the individual for corporately assigned tasks, heals hurts, comforts (strengthens) the weakhearted. Group dynamism can serve good or evil causes. Rival dynamisms confront each other. Insight into the miracle-working powers of group solidarity can give meaning to the New Testament description of the church's struggle against the demonic forces arrayed against it in the ancient world — among them " the *spirit* that is now at work in the sons of disobedience" (Eph. 2:2, italics mine). Our battle, says this same letter, is "not . . . against flesh and blood, but against the principalities, against the powers, against the world rulers of this present darkness, against the spiritual hosts of wickedness in the heavenly places" (Eph. 6:12).

Into the complexity of New Testament cosmology and its picture of angelic powers we cannot enter here, though it may be said in passing that the study of group life may throw much light upon this puzzling area of New Testament symbolism. Sufficient for our purpose may be allusion to the fact that the analogy of spirit powers resident in every group solidarity may be of help in understanding the event of Pentecost. The peculiar power imparted to the Christian community at Pentecost came also in the form of *spirit* — now, however, the Holy Spirit. The individual Christian receives the gift of this empowering Spirit at Baptism when he is incorporated into the fellowship which is Christ's "body," and of which the Spirit is, as it were, the soul. And the gift of the Spirit implies the imparting of power — the original Greek word for power being precisely *dynamis*, yielding our English words "dynamic" and "dynamics." If, consequently, in the communal life of the Pentecostal fellowship we look for analogies to the powers resident in group solidarities outside the church, or alongside the church, or even as demonic rivals of the church, we are clearly not disappointed. In the church, however, these powers are in the service of Christ, the church's Lord, not of "the prince of this world" (John 14:30), or of a mere human idealism. No secular group power, even when it lives on derivative Christian grace and is, in our western democratic social order not yet, we trust, under the rule of demonic "principalities," can touch more than a fringe of basic human needs. It breaks under the strain.

Gratitude, accordingly, for what our social scientists are contributing toward a recovery of insight into the latent powers resident in Christian community life, must not lose sight of an ultimate gulf between "church" and "world." Our secular associations and the hundreds of fellowships that nightly fill meeting halls in our American towns and cities still live, as just admitted, on a residuum of Christian grace. Yet, in final analysis, do they not one and all depend for their initial uniting power on some form of exclusion? Group isolation (one thinks of the average country club) is still isolation. Acceptance of one candidate for membership normally implies rejection of another — and such rejection can bring on itself the corporate guilt of murder. Suicide as response to failure to be accepted in a college fraternity is not unknown. Furthermore, without belittling in the least the benefits by way of receiving recognition as a person which even an exclusive group can bestow, can it abolish the poison of envy or jealousy in the hearts of its members? Can it heal a broken marriage, or, when family crises appear, can it "turn the hearts of fathers to their children and the hearts of children to their fathers"? All ultimate chasms between man and man analyzed in an earlier chapter remain as they were.

And when the relationship between man and God is involved, " group dynamics " is wholly impotent. It can tell us much of the gift of group acceptance and the loneliness of group rejection. It does not presume to speak of the loneliness of guilt, of the agony of a sin-laden conscience, or of the grace of divine forgiveness. Indeed, expectations of what group " togetherness " can accomplish can very quickly encounter disillusionment. The very word " togetherness " has become shopworn and is arousing at times cynical response — a reaction that has not left such experience in fellowship revival as once motivated the Oxford Group Movement, or even Alcoholics Anonymous untouched. " Groupiness " is already a derisive term.[59]

Nevertheless, our churches stand under judgment. Pietistic individualism, on either Roman Catholic or Protestant soil, did not reveal its weakness in days when the average Christian was still surrounded by a community life in village or town nourished by the charity of the gospel. The powers of the Holy Spirit performed their healing and strengthening tasks in the Christian family and in the closely knit Christian community throughout the week, and were not dependent for finding avenues of expression solely upon a formalized worship on Sunday. The latter could be safely formalized and did not need to revert to the primitive fellowship meeting of the church of New Testament times.

Our problem is the reverse of that confronting our forefathers. For us the problem consists of recreating, within and alongside the church's institutional activities, the Christian community in which Christian charity can bring to men and women the gift of the glorious liberty of the children of God. For if we turn for a vision of what Christian fellowship might be when true to the norm of the New Testament, the wonder and glory of the *koinōnia Spiritu Sancti* leaps to life. Here, where " there is neither Jew nor Greek, there is neither slave nor free, there is neither male nor female; for you are all one in Christ Jesus" (Gal. 3:28), exclusion is apostasy. Here is a brotherhood of penitence and gratitude. Here the Spirit power at work is not one engendered in a frail human group trusting in its own ability to free captives of isolation or to bring the gift of human dignity to victims of mass dehumanization, but God himself. Here is a "colony of heaven" in the midst of a dying world, one that enjoys a foretaste of a new heaven and earth beyond mortality's dread end. Indeed, it would require a paraphrase of chapter after chapter of the New Testament to describe even partially the miracle of the emergence in history of the Kingdom of Christ.

Whenever and wherever the church manifests itself as truly this "new being," a community of men and women resurrected from the dead, is there any question that its very existence is already a witness to the gospel, thus sharing in Christ's mission to the world? How else can the historian explain the march of the mission across the Roman world in the church's great apostolic era? "What a sense of stability a creation of this kind must have conferred upon the individual!" So the noted historian Adolf Harnack describes that mission's march. "What powers of attraction," he continues, "it must have exercised, as soon as its objects came to be understood! It was this, and not any evangelist, which proved to be the most effective missionary. In fact, we may take it as an assured fact that the mere existence and persistent activity of the individual Christian communities did more than anything else to bring about the extension of the Christian religion." [60]

But questions inevitably arise as we submit many a congregation as we know it to the judgment of such a vision. Where are the fellowships to be found that manifest this power of witness? An indictment has been voiced in earlier paragraphs against the self-worshiping church for its failure to accept the call to mission beyond its borders. A parallel indictment could frequently be voiced against a congregation's witness *within* its borders. This indictment already projected in the presentation of group dynamics analogies could take various forms. We could listen with profit, for example, to John Wesley as, even two hundred years ago, he lamented the absence of Christian fellowship in his own still beloved Church of England:

Christian fellowship, where is it to be found? Look east or west, north or south; name what parish you please: Is this Christian fellowship there? Rather, are not the bulk of parishioners a mere rope of sand? What Christian connection is there between them? What intercourse in spiritual things? What watching over each other's souls? What bearing of one another's burdens? [61]

An equally penetrating question, however, also looms on the horizon: What are the boundaries of this community of the resurrection? Is there a boundary in God's design short of all mankind? In a sense surely not violating wholly a concept of the church as God must view it, all men are already "in Christ" and "in the church." God's reconciliation of the world to himself in Christ embraces every child born of woman. The church is not a community of the saved as contrasted with the lost in so far as availability of grace is concerned. One of the Johannine letters can remind us that Jesus Christ, as "advocate with the Father," is indeed "the expiation for our sins," yet "not for ours only but also for the sins of the whole world" (I John 2:1-2). We who have heard the gospel and are enjoying its benefits resemble a few members of a large family who happen to have been present when a testament (that great word on the title page of our Bible) was read with its news of a rich inheritance. Absent members of the family, however, are clearly meant to share its wealth equally with ourselves. Can we, the privileged few, calmly enjoy our share and take prior possession of the family mansion before the absent members have so much as heard the news of their equal rights and privileges?

The analogy might be carried even farther. There might be a clause in the testamentary document withholding all but a fractional distribution of the family fortune until the family has been reunited, its prodigal sons receiving the joyous welcome of a reunion feast.

"All analogies," so reads a Jesuit proverb, "walk on three legs." The one just sketched is obviously only a groping toward a full vision of the church's vocation as both end and means in God's design. An invitation to prodigal sons to return home would be meaningless if there were no home to which to return. Precisely because the church here and now is already a sacrament of the Kingdom, it can be an instrument for the spread of the gospel meant for all mankind. It witnesses to itself. But woe unto a church that transforms this witness into enjoyment of unearned privilege. It has no right as yet to a permanent Sabbath rest.

During the era of "foreign missions" of the past few centuries, when at least a remnant within the churches took the missionary vocation seriously, no text of the New Testament had a greater motivating power for the gospel's march across lands and oceans than Matt. 24:14 — greater even, so some historians of missions tell us, than the more familiar closing verse of that Gospel, "Go therefore and make disciples of all nations." The earlier verse reads: "And this gospel of the kingdom will be preached throughout the whole world, as a testimony to all nations; and then the end will come." This verse surely deserves resurrection as charter once more for both church and missions as they reunite for a renewed obedience to the church's Lord. This fourteenth verse of the twenty-fourth chapter of the Gospel of Matthew has its setting in Christ's preview of the Kingdom's consummation. The disciples press him for an answer to their question: "What will be the sign of your coming and of the close of the age?" What follows is the unforgettable picture of the trials that await the Kingdom's witnesses and martyrs. The prophecy's climax is the vision of the church's mission. The end, prayed for by the early church with its cry "Come, Lord Jesus," must await that mission's fulfillment — a mission devolving on Christ's disciples until the end of time. For this great missionary prophecy is addressed to us as it was to the apostolic band.

The church, like an army, is indeed privileged between campaigns to enjoy rest and refreshment. But it remains, even in its hours of rejoicing and thanksgiving for the gospel's victories, on call for renewed mission service. That mission's end is not yet. There will be a day of judgment before the creation of a new heaven and a new earth. Can we ignore the awesome fact of that Day of Judgment?

"He comes again," so we sing in one of our familiar hymns:

> He comes again: O Zion, ere thou meet him,
> Make known to every heart his saving grace;
> Let none whom he hath ransomed fail to greet him,
> Through thy neglect, unfit to see his face.

"Unfit to see his face" — the hymn writer may have had in mind the "unfitness" of those who as yet have not heard the redemptive message of the gospel. But the word may be even more applicable to us if we have been unfaithful servants. "Not every one who says to me, 'Lord, Lord,' shall enter the kingdom of heaven, but he who does the will of my Father who is in heaven." (Matt. 7:21.)

Chapter V

The Witness of the Scattered People of God

Where is the church? If this question were asked in our hearing, we might be puzzled to find a ready answer. We might, in fact, suggest that no one asks this question, not at least in the lands of the older Christendom. *The* church? There is no such "church" in the singular in our communities. We only know "churches," or *a* church, or *the* Lutheran, *the* Episcopal, or *the* Baptist church. The disunity existing among the "churches" burdens the very word "church" with a tragic ambiguity. If, however, we substitute for the word "church" one of the symbols or images that are synonyms for "church" in the Bible, namely, the phrase "the people of God," the question, Where is the church? ceases to be quite so embarrassing. No denominational church (not even the exclusive Church of Rome) boasts of monopoly rights to this Scriptural definition of those who bear the name of Christ. The image of the church as "the people of God" approaches the inclusiveness of the even simpler term "Christians."

Nevertheless, an ambiguity burdens the image "people of God" also. The Greek word for people is *laos;* this has become our English word "laity." "Laity," in turn, has stolen a march on the corporate meaning of "people of God," monopolizing it for those members of the churches who are not office-bearers. The latter, if thought of as a separate caste or order or hierarchy or as "the ministry" of the church, are, so it seems, excluded. Some Protestant doctrines of the church are tempted

101

to say: "Let them remain excluded, at least insofar as giving them rights over the laity is involved. We need no priesthood in the church except the priesthood of all believers." At the opposite end of the doctrinal spectrum, as we all know, is the hierarchical ministry of the Roman Church. The laity, under this view, are, in their turn almost excluded from the church.

"The church," so reads a pronouncement of Pope Pius X, "is the mystical body of Christ, a body ruled by pastors and teachers, a society of men headed by rulers having full and perfect powers of governing, instructing, and judging. It follows that this church is essentially two categories of persons; pastors and the flock; those who hold rank in different degrees of the hierarchy and the multitude of the faithful. And these categories are so distinct in themselves that in the pastoral body alone resides the necessary right and authority to guide and direct all the members toward the goal of the society. As for the multitude, it has no other right than that of allowing itself to be led, and, as a docile flock, to follow its shepherds." [62]

Any definitive "theology of the laity" would have to deal at length with this gulf between Protestant and Roman Catholic doctrines of the church and the ministry and of the place of the laity within the inclusive body of Christ. I make no pretense of entering the lists in this theological warfare. For my purposes, I limit myself to a few modest footnotes to the dialogue.

As an Anglican, I am convinced that neither the "hierarchical church" nor the "lay church" — to employ shorthand designations — can bear the test of submission to the norm of the New Testament. One of Anglicanism's modern doctrinal "classics" is clearly in line with the New Testament evidence when it points out that the church began with a "distinction corresponding to that drawn later between clergy and laity" already in existence — an apostolate and a body of believers. "There was not first an apostolate which gathered a body of believers about itself; nor was there a completely structureless collection of believers which gave authority to the apostles to speak and act on its behalf." The development within the church of a shepherding and even priestly ministry, accordingly, looks to an Anglican as only to be expected, provided that this remains a representative priesthood. "The fundamental priesthood of the church is thus the priesthood of the whole body. This is the meaning of the doctrine of the priesthood of the laity, a doctrine which does not mean that laymen are individually priests, but that the laity are, as such, members of the body which is in its entirety priestly." [63]

Having thus eased my conscience by way of citing at least one ameliorating view of the Roman Catholic–Protestant doctrinal conflict, I venture on a second observation — one that may also suggest that a growth of mutual understanding is possible between the two traditions. A Protestant layman is undoubtedly shocked when he meets a description of his supposed status in the church like the one held by Pius X. But is he, the Protestant layman, ready to accept and to activate the more exalted status which, in theory, his tradition accords him? He views the sacerdotal monopoly of powers in the Romanist world with aversion. But substitute for the word "sacerdotalism" the cognate word "clericalism," and he may be given pause. The ministerial power figure in the Protestant tradition has moved, let us say, from the altar to the pulpit. But is the ministry in its new location any less in danger of being accorded monopoly rights? It is now, however, the laity, not a papal fiat, which crowns the ministry with a status halo. It is far easier to hand over the burden of evangelism and pastoral care — which, according to the doctrine of the priesthood of all believers devolves on every church member — to certain professional Christians who are paid to perform them.

One of the popular uses of the word "layman" is illustrated in much Protestant church life. In current usage in medicine, law, and many other technical fields, "lay" means unlearned and unqualified. It comes close to meaning ignorant. When the laity in the churches are content to let *ignorance* determine their status in the church, clericalism is inevitable. "For many

Protestants," so reads a confession in a recent study of the Protestant ministry in America, "the ministry is very nearly the whole church, and the minister is the ' preacher.' " [64] Yves Congar, whose monumental work, *Lay People in the Church*, is an invaluable survey, though from the Romanist side, of "today's problem of a theology of the laity," reminds Protestants that, although "starting from strict congregationalist premises and an associational and community basis, they are in practice almost as clericalized as the Catholic Church." [65] If clericalism is wrong, both Protestants and Roman Catholics have a problem on their hands.

My third observation will, I trust, lead directly to the main theme of this chapter. This theme is not an attempt to contribute more than a few footnotes toward " a theology of the laity." Congar's book just cited and a volume coming from the Protestant world, Hendrik Kraemer's *A Theology of the Laity*,[66] are already proof that this is a subject calling for the devotion to it of major theological talent. Touch the theology of the laity and you are plunged at once into wrestling with a theology of the ministry, of the sacraments, and of the church — the entire circle of themes which underlie the problems of church unity and which the ecumenical movement is exploring. Fortunately, awakening the churches of whatever name and tradition to the call to evangelism and mission does not have to wait until church unity has been achieved or until the problem of church order has been resolved. As world and church confront each other and a dialogue ensues, the world cares very little, initially at least, whether the witness to the gospel is a Roman Catholic or a Protestant. What Protestant and Roman Catholic have in common by way of basic belief in God and his revelation of himself in the Biblical salvation drama far transcends their differences. The word " Christian " still has an ecumenically inclusive meaning.

I return now, after this brief look at the implications of the word "laity," to the question at the head of this chapter: Where is the church? When we take seriously the image of the church as the *laos*, the people of God, an answer to this question can lead us far. The question, Where is the church? can find an answer also in the image of the church employed in the previous chapter: " You are the salt of the earth." Salt, we recall, appears in two forms, as gathered salt and as scattered salt. If, when we ask, " Where is the church? " we think first of the gathered people of God — gathered on one day of the week — the answer is easy. The church is precisely " in church." There it manifests itself corporately as what it is, the body of Christ, " Christ in community." But the church as people of God does not cease to exist when its members have left the church building. They are now, however, throughout the workaday week, the scattered salt of the Kingdom, the scattered people of God.

The argument of the opening chapter deserves review here. This was a plea for acceptance on the part of Christians of an incarnational, or secular, evangelism, for witnessing to Christ in the workaday world where men and women actually live. The phrase " church in world " — a translation of *Kerk en Wereld*, the name of an evangelizing new life center in Holland — can symbolize this fresh stirring of conscience in the churches in our time. When such consciousness of the church as mission comes alive, the first impulse, however, is to find a special agency of the church, a home missions department, perhaps, to which this evangelizing task can be assigned. Clericalism, though this may now receive an institutional enlargement so as to involve clericalized laymen as well as the ordained ministry, is still not dislodged. By all means, so we are tempted to plead, let us support a hospital, or a community center, chaplains for penal institutions, and mission stations in the slums; this, if well done, fulfills our obligation. What is needed is the shock of discovering that obedience to the call to mission in the world needs no special evangelizing agencies, useful as these may be. The church *is* already *in* the world. The " where? " of the church as scattered people of God is precisely outside church walls.

A paragraph in the Report of the Evanston Assembly of the World Council of Churches (1954) gives to this simple fact vivid expression:

The real battles of faith today are being fought in factories, shops, offices, and farms, in political parties and government agencies, in countless homes, in the press, radio, and television, in the relationship of nations. Very often it is said that the church should " go into these spheres," but the fact is that the church *is* already in these spheres in the persons of its laity.[67]

A further surprise, or even shock, awaits us if we ask in which of the two manifestations of the church — as the gathered people of God or as the scattered people of God — the Christian layman finds his normal habitat. The answer is obvious: in the scattered church. We are so accustomed to think of the church as *really* the church only when it is " in church," that we are tempted to deposit the consciousness of *being the church* on our local meetinghouse doorstep when we leave at the close of a Sunday service. We shall then, of course, pick it up again when another Sunday comes round.

We need, consequently, repeated reminders of the fact that the people of God are " church " and " body of Christ " not merely one or two hours a week. Dietrich Bonhoeffer, whose prophetic insights have served, by way of quotation, to buttress the argument of this book more than once already, can again be called up as a witness. One of his most appealing writings is his *Life Together,* a description of the joy and wonder of the Christian's experience in the gathered manifestation of the church. It is, indeed, almost a manual of a revived monasticism, proof that incarnational evangelism must have a Christ to carry out into the world who has first been experienced as " Christ in community." Yet Bonhoeffer opens his book with a warning that " life together " is granted to the Christian only as a privilege and a gift of grace, and not as a right that relieves him of his real vocation, namely, witnessing to his faith in the world. I cite an excerpt from Bonhoeffer's opening paragraphs:

It is not simply to be taken for granted that the Christian has the privilege of living with other Christians. Jesus Christ lived in the midst of his enemies. On the cross he was utterly alone, surrounded by evildoers and mockers. For this cause he had come, to bring peace to the enemies of God. So the Christian, too, belongs not in the seclusion of a cloistered life, but in the thick of foes. There is his commission, his work. " The Kingdom is to be in the midst of your enemies. And he who will not suffer this does not want to be of the Kingdom of Christ; he wants to be among friends, to sit among roses and lilies, not with the bad people but with devout people. O you blasphemers and betrayers of Christ! If Christ had done what you are doing, who would ever have been spared? " (Luther.)

According to God's will Christendom is a scattered people, scattered like seed " into all the kingdoms of the earth " (Deut. 28:25). That is its curse and its promise. God's people must dwell in far countries among unbelievers, but it will be the seed of the Kingdom of God in all the world.

So between the death of Christ and the Last Day, it is only by a gracious anticipation of the last things that Christians are privileged to live in visible fellowship with other Christians.[68]

In the discussion in the preceding chapter of the church's basic vocation as mission, the analogy of a Copernican revolution proved of use. A church true to its vocation as on mission sent is called upon to surrender its institutional self-worship and to become servant to a gospel meant for all mankind. The need of a Copernican revolution may appear on the horizon also as we try to gain a right view of the relationship between the gathered and the scattered people of God. It may prove to be especially pertinent in throwing light on the respective vocations of *the* ministry (the office-bearing caste) and the church's lay membership. The word " ministry " means simply " serving "; and minister means " servant." This is one of the basic concepts of the New Testament, descriptive of Christ's own vocation, and thus it devolves upon his disciples (Mark 9:35; cf. Rom. 1:1). Every Christian, by virtue of having been commissioned in Baptism as " Christ's faithful soldier and ser-

vant," participates in his Lord's ministry. This is a doctrinal commonplace. Yet the temptation to clericalize the word " ministry " by placing the article " the " before it and thus removing it from general application is almost irresistible.

The Department on the Laity of the World Council of Churches has enjoyed a kind of theological thrill in correcting the misunderstanding which has resulted from a faulty translation of one of the key " evangelism " texts of the New Testament, at least in English versions, because of that little article " the." The story of an overdue emendation in that text may be important enough to deserve retelling. The text is Eph. 4:11-12. In the King James Version this reads, the subject of the sentence being the ascended Christ: " And he gave some, apostles; and some, prophets; and some, evangelists; and some, pastors and teachers; for the perfecting of the saints, for the work of the ministry, for the edifying of the body of Christ." A corrected translation — the Revised Standard Version gives it to us — omits the article " the " before " ministry." If read afresh, " ministry " now describes a function and an activity, and not a special order in the church. The passage can then serve as basis for the Copernican revolution suggested as needful in the previous paragraph. *The* ministry now has no monopoly in " building up [RSV for " edifying of "] the body of Christ," the laity presumably those being edified or built up, or at best supporting *the* ministry by way of what we think of as laymen's church work.

Such laymen's church work is not ruled out, of course. Some of the " gifts " of the Lord to the church may be precisely lay vocations. The word " teachers " certainly enlarges the roster of callings to " church work " by wide margins. Many more lay callings for " in church " service readily come to mind. But we miss the point of the passage if we pause there. The real " work of ministry " is to be the vocation of the " saints," a word used in the New Testament to describe all members of the church. The function of the shepherding leadership of the church is to " perfect " these " saints " for their mission. In other words, the laity are the ultimate bearers of the church's ministerial vocation. The shepherds of the flock — apostles, prophets, evangelists, teachers — have a vocation also, of course. But instead of their assuming ministerial monopoly rights, the laity mere acolytes or assistants, the assignment of such monopoly rights, if indeed such there be, is virtually reversed. The shepherding group now become the acolytes and assistants.

It would be an irresponsible reading of the New Testament to push this Copernican revolution paradox too far. After all, the clerical orders in the church are also members of the people of God — the "other laity" as they have been called. Their specialized vocations are essential to the very existence of a people of God in the first place. But when the pope in the Roman Church proudly wears the title "Servant of the servants of God," this has profound meaning for a theology both of the ministry and of the laity. And since allusion has been made to the great Church of Rome, attention could be called to the literally astounding acceptance on the part of Roman Catholic theologians during recent generations of a radical reappraisal of the traditional monopoly rights of the hierarchy.

Hendrik Kraemer's A Theology of the Laity quotes a sentence of Pope Pius XII's which he finds surprising, but which is echoed in much other present-day Romanist ecclesiology. The sentence reads: "The laity are the church; they make the church." [69] When Karl Barth, in a masterful portrayal of how every Christian participates in Christ's ministry, summarily says, "The life of the children of God is simply the life of the church of God," [70] a strange Protestant–Roman Catholic consensus on this issue of church and mission looms on the horizon.

Protestants could envy Rome for giving prominence to the striking phrase "the apostolate of the laity," to designate the laity's evangelizing vocation. The connotation surrounding the words "apostle" and "apostolic" are thus rescued from imprisonment in a hierarchical context (Anglicans please note!) and given functional meaning. Congar, for whose explorations into a theology of the laity all of us can be repeatedly grateful, accords rights to "the baptismal priesthood of the faithful" [71] (a doctrine he finds clearly expressed even in the *Summa* of Thomas Aquinas) which may exceed in practical manifestation those which are supposedly the exclusive prerogative of the priesthood of all believers of Protestant ecclesiology. More than one prophet of things to come in our ecumenical era predicts that obedience to the call to mission will open unexpected pathways to Christian unity. "For the Lord will rise up . . . to do his deed — strange is his deed! and to work his work — alien is his work!" (Isa. 28:21.)

So much by way of background for exploring in at least some detail the vocation of the scattered people of God. The laity have been called the frozen assets of the church. How can those who suffer from such glacial burial be unfrozen, and how can they be equipped and perfected for "the work of ministry" to which their baptismal priesthood calls them?

One of the first needs, surely, is to rouse in all members of the body of Christ — laity and "other laity" alike — a realization of what they are. Even when we are asked to manifest the reality of the body of Christ as a gathered people of God, how lightly this calling rests upon our conscience! Our Romanist brethren are still taught that absence from the weekly gathering of the faithful at mass is mortal sin — sin with deadly consequences. The legalism of this ecclesiastical discipline may deserve some of the questioning which Protestants find it easy to voice. But has the obligation to take seriously membership in the body of Christ been abrogated for those not under Romanist rule? I recall the shock of conscience I experienced in coming almost by chance upon a passage in an early church document which gives deep theological meaning to such a simple act as church attendance. "When thou teachest," so reads the homily, "command and remind the people that they be constant in the assembly of the church; so that ye be not hindered and make smaller by a member the body of Christ. Do not deprive our Savior of his members; Do not mangle and scatter his body." [72] Staying away from church sounds innocent. Mangling and scattering the body of Christ has the trumpet sound of Judgment Day!

An analogy from military life may be helpful here. An army regiment normally becomes a "gathered" military unit only periodically at a parade mount or review when the commanding officer issues his general orders and when even the lowest-ranking private experiences the uniting power of the regiment's *esprit de corps.* But what would be left of such *esprit* if the commanding officer faced a regiment on review of whose membership roster only a third or at most a half were graciously willing to appear at all, the remainder turning a review day into a holiday?

If the conscience of the lay members of the body of Christ needs to be awakened to the awesome meaning of their membership in the gathered church, a similar awakening of conscience awaits them when the corresponding significance of membership in the scattered church looms on the horizon. The analogy from military life may prove useful here also, since the laity's baptismal priesthood has made them soldiers of Christ. Presence at a regimental review is, in a soldier's life, only a small fraction of military duty, and, indeed, of his training in the military life. If a soldier received no schooling for his calling other than voluntary appearance at a weekly parade, a nation trusting in such guardians would be in sorry plight. Yet this is the state of many a congregation's equipment for Christian warfare against "sin, the world, and the devil."

Every analogy runs into the law of limits. But, insofar as this parable taken from military life can throw light on the vocation of the laity in the church, one subsidiary application leaps to the eye. The Christian soldier, like his secular counterpart, has to receive training for his vocation not solely, or even first of all, on the parade ground. The primary training school of an army is the squad and the platoon. Corporals and sergeants are as indispensable in the life of a regiment as is the commissioned officers' corps.

Churches throughout the world are in our era rediscovering the importance for the training of the Christian layman for his witnessing vocation of precisely the "squad" and the "platoon." These training schools are not given these names, to be sure, but the realities are analogous. We speak more frequently of Christian "cells" — a biological metaphor made meaningful by the New Testament image of the church as body. John Wesley is being recognized, belatedly by Anglicans, but by other traditions as well, as one of the church's wisest statesmen. His clear insight into the failure of the institutionalized church of his day to supplement "parade ground" training with a discipline possible only in "squad" or "platoon" led him to enroll the laity under his charge in what were called "classes" — small groups under the care of lay leadership, but a leadership that had received special training for a "corporal's" or "sergeant's" role. The "class meeting" — a midweek gathering of Christians for fellowship and mutual encouragement in witnessing to their faith in daily life — was the glory also of traditional Congregationalism. The story of what happened to this manifestation of "the equipment of the saints for the work of ministry" since those earlier days cannot be told here. Suffice it to say that rediscovery of its profound value is spreading throughout the Christian world. Fr. Congar hails the revival of community or fellowship Christianity in his own communion as a long-needed corrective to its temptation to deny to the laity an experience of church life in which "the religious subject is personally and communally active." [73]

It ought to be a cause for shame on the part of both Protestants and Roman Catholics that the very concept of the church as a fellowship in which every member glories in the "gift of tongues," with the privilege of mutual dialogue and sharing of burdens and receiving help for his witnessing vocation in the world has lain fallow so long. All that would have been needed to bring realization that something was missing in an institutionalized Christianity in which the clerical monologue had monopoly rights was a recalling to mind of the norm of the

New Testament ecclesia. A reading of Paul's description of the church of Corinth could have brought correctives: "When you come together, each one has a hymn, a lesson, a revelation, a tongue, or an interpretation. . . . Let two or three prophets speak, and let the others weigh what is said. . . . For you can all prophesy one by one, so that all may learn and all be encouraged" (I Cor. 14:26, 29, 31).

When has the average layman in our churches (I write as an Anglican) ever experienced "church" in this manifestation? Each member of the church, lay as well as clerical, is to be permitted to voice a revelation and to prophesy? This would be unheard of. It might create alarms and revolutions in our decorous middle-class assemblies! Paul, too, is aware of dangers in granting such freedom to often still immature Christians. He counsels that "all things should be done decently and in order" (I Cor. 14:40). But he underscores the right to liberty of speech despite the risks. "So, my brethren, earnestly desire to prophesy, and do not forbid speaking in tongues." [74] (I Cor. 14:39.)

A whole chapter would have to be devoted to describing even in brief outline the ways in which the experience of Christian fellowship in small groups is in our time receiving new emphasis. A bibliography alone could cover pages. The title of one of the many books descriptive of this recovery gives a clue to what this "cell movement," as it is frequently called, has in view. The book is *Spiritual Renewal Through Personal Groups,* by John L. Casteel. A pamphlet issued by the Laity Department of the World Council of Churches (1956) gives a picture of the ministry of the lay institutes which are flourishing in Europe under the title *Signs of Renewal,* the phrase prophetic of things still to come. Another volume that describes these institutes is *Bridges to Understanding,* by Margaret Frakes.[75]

Ernest W. Southcott, of Leeds, England, in *The Parish Comes Alive,*[76] gives an account of how the House-church Movement, so-called, brought life to an ossified parish in Great Britain. I enjoyed the privilege of a visit in Canon Southcott's parish and can testify to the amazing effect that freeing the experience of "church" from imprisonment in traditional Gothic walls can produce. "Where is the church of Halton, Leeds?" "On Monday morning, it will be at number 21 Devonshire Street, where a Communion service will be held in a cottage kitchen and parlor." The House-church Movement has a service to perform on the English scene, perhaps, which is not so needed in America, since the "church in four walls" has not become suspect with us quite as it has in Europe. Yet with us, too, supplementation of Sunday formal worship by way of meetings of lay people in small groups has much promise. Such meetings can become evangelizing agencies of unique influence and power. Not only can the faithful "renew their strength" (Isa. 40:31), but outsiders who are not ready for incorporation into the gathered church can be given their first intimation of what life together in a Christian fellowship can mean.

Such informal gatherings of Christians in free dialogue with non-Christians are sometimes called, in the current literature of evangelism, "halfway churches" or "para-churches," or "way stations" on the road to full participation in the life of the baptized. Here the miracle of receiving the dignity of being a person with a name and being rescued from the depersonalized anonymity of our urban society can happen. "Massification or isolation: that is the common choice which lies before most people today" [77] — so many Christian sociologists describe our common secular life. Many potential converts must be given an experience of a third possibility — in the fellowship of the Holy Spirit — before ears will be opened to hear the gospel itself.

The importance for evangelism of these "little churches" received eloquent underscoring in one of the reports — by the Section on Witness — of the Assembly of the World Council of Churches at New Delhi. The passage reads:

It may be that the local church should seek to penetrate into the unevangelized population by the setting up of "cells" or local Christian community groups: a handful of typists and salesgirls in a big store; a dozen or so workers on the various floors of a factory; eight research workers and their wives in a big chemical plant; a few Christian teachers on the staff of a big school; a little congregation gathered from two or three streets, meeting as a house-church in the home of one of their number. They will try to be the church, the people of God, in their own particular context.

And if concern arises over the danger that such fragmentation of a congregation will rob the gathered church of its corporate ministry, the report has this to say:

Eventually the local church buildings might function as the centers to which all these groups might come, not destroying their fellowship or their own way of witness, as a "congregation of congregations," witnessing to the reality of the whole church to which they all belong and the Lord of all life in whom all human categories and classes are made one.[78]

The reader may have noted, however, that if the ministry of the scattered salt of the Kingdom is our theme, the presentation of what this may mean has itself halted at a way station. Meetings of lay people in small groups are still a manifestation of the gathered people of God. Ultimately the life of the Christian must turn into a witnessing vocation without even these corporate protections. He may be on lonely outpost in his daily environment, no squad leader or fellow soldier of Christ anywhere near. How can he be a witness in this situation? This is a question that causes anxiety to many an earnest layman. He may well be reminded that his most effective witness to and communication of the gospel may come by way of his simplest contacts with his fellows, rather than through any overtly "religious" activities. "The very nature of our being," says Harry A. DeWire, "is defined in terms of communication. Hardly any aspect of the physical or psychological makeup is free from involvement in the give-and-take with the world."[79] This fact ought to be obvious. Yet we are, surely, surprised again and again when we discover that even an unconscious gesture has been a communication of our faith in God or of our lapse into unbelief.

We witness by what we wear and by the way we walk or by a chance meeting on a street corner. Karl Barth, in a moving exposition of what obedience to the command to love our neighbor implies, brings this home to Christian conscience:

To speak to our neighbor about Jesus Christ and to show him brotherly love appear at first sight to be realizable possibilities. But what can I do to ensure that the picture which I offer in my person is evangelical and not heathen or legal? What can I do about the disposition and mood and atmosphere which I spread? " The redeemed must look redeemed." Here in this question of attitude (*Haltung* in the German), more clearly than in that of word or deed, we are reminded that the task appointed us in this time and world, to praise God and love our neighbor, demands more than an isolated doing — it demands the whole life.[80]

Karl Barth is voicing a counsel of perfection that none of us can hear without being led to an act of penitence and a prayer for assistance from a Power far beyond our own. Yet the first lesson that those of us who are the scattered salt of the Kingdom need to learn is precisely the almost limitless dimension of the witnessing opportunities of Christians. And if this insight burdens conscience, it can also bring release from many tensions and from overly anxious and premature attempts to convert our neighbors. Karl Barth alludes to " speaking to our neighbor about Jesus Christ." The supposition that a layman is failing in communicating the gospel unless he has a miniature sermon ready to hand has done, on occasion, great harm. The neighbor may be far from ready for the sermon. The layman, in turn, may as yet not have won the right to be heard. The eager layman can afford to relax. Witnessing is not going by default if conversation with a neighbor remains on a secular plane and even shuns every religious allusion.

We could recall here the three steps in communication cited in a previous chapter as having proved helpful in evangelizing strategy in France: *présence, service, communication*. Presence! This alone — the enduring of human presence — if motivated by Christian grace, is already a harbinger of the gospel. We like distance between us and our neighbor, since hell, for unredeemed man, is still "other people." Presence, accordingly, is not easy. Can we suppose that the Jesus of the Gospel story found it easy to dine with publicans and sinners? We can find in the book of Ezekiel, prophet of Israel in exile, a confession of what such an experience can mean. "Then I came to them of the captivity of Tel-abib, that dwelt by the river of Chebar, and I sat where they sat, and remained there astonished among them seven days." (Ezek. 3:15.) Most of us could testify that we have been in situations in which mere "presence" was not only astonishing but almost unendurable. Many missionaries have broken under the burden.

Add to the evangelizing ministry of "presence" that of service, and we may still be helping to prepare our neighbor for the hearing of the gospel. Is this what our Lord had in mind when, in the great Sermon, he bids his disciples to walk a second mile, to turn the other cheek, and to give to him who begs? Walking, too, can come hard — simply walking, with possibly no word spoken, at the side of a neighbor in need, hungry for the grace of a caring friend. These are all instances of nonverbal communication of the gospel, but how significant they can become! Related to them is the ministry of listening — obviously nonverbal. This too is not easy, since listening, by its very nature, can be threatening. "We are not sure of the demands it will bring, nor what we shall do with the demands that do come. To listen is to have our souls open to attack." [81]

To realize the evangelizing power of mere "presence" is not easy for most of us. We are so accustomed to think of the call to spread the gospel as one demanding primarily some kind of verbal witness — talking to a neighbor about Jesus — that mere presence looks like shirking our witnessing task. Yet missionary experience can bring much testimony to bear that premature attempts to achieve conversions can do more harm than good.

One of the outstanding examples of a missionary who found his vocation as one of mere presence, with all that this involved by way of silent yet sacrificial evangelism, is the by now famous Charles de Foucauld, founder of the Roman Catholic order of the Little Brothers of Jesus. Charles de Foucauld dedicated his life to being a missionary to the Moslem world, in particular to the Touareg peoples in the Sahara. Islam is notoriously resistant to Christianity, and De Foucauld was under no illusion that he would see a quick harvest of converts. He simply lived in the midst of the Touareg people. " His vocation," so one of his biographers describes it, " was one of being *present* among people, with a presence willed and intended as a witness of the love of Christ. . . . He *became* a Touareg to the depth of his soul. I mean that he completely gave himself to these people, not only spiritually, but humanly; for he well knew how intimately the Christian life is bound up with the whole context of life." [82] One of his own reports on his missionary activity reads simply as follows:

I help as far as I can; I try to show that I love. When the opportunity seems favorable, I speak of natural religion, of God's commandments, of his love, of union with his will and love of one's neighbors. Ignorant as they are, they can receive the gospel only by authority, and the authority necessary to make them adopt it and reject all they know, love and venerate, can only be acquired after long and intimate contact, by great virtue and God's blessing.

Charles de Foucauld envisaged the ongoing mission to Islamic people by fellow missionaries who followed him as pioneer as one again of patient " presence."

It will be a work of time, demanding self-sacrifice, character, and constancy. We want good priests (not to preach: they would be received as Turks coming to preach Mahomet would be received in Breton villages), but to establish contact, to make themselves loved, to inspire esteem, trust, and friendship. . . . That being done, conversions at the end of twenty-five, fifty, or a hundred years will come of themselves as fruit ripens.[83]

To wait twenty-five to one hundred years for the " fruit " of evangelism, with no preaching permitted — this certainly is a

revolutionary vision of gospel witnessing. Nor need the special
vocation of missionary work in Islamic countries become a
model for all evangelism at home, though more than one so-
called industrial mission in our European and American cities
is willing to face similar trials of patience and of waiting long
for a conversion harvest.[84] Nevertheless, even on a small scale,
when a layman submits himself to the call of being a witness
for Christ, the power of presence and "being a Christian" can
receive much validation. Florence Allshorn, a missionary of
much experience in Africa, relates in her *Notebooks* an incident that might well be pondered by all of us who are only too
prone to think of Christian evangelism as a failure when it is
not "up and doing." She tells of a young officer in the British
Armed Forces who said to a Christian: "Don't try to help me
or preach to me, or tell me what I ought to think yet. Don't
work for my salvation, show me yours, show me it is possible,
and the knowledge that something works will give me courage
and belief in mine."[85]

The author of a recent book on the missionary challenge of
our time, who cites the just related incident, adds a comment
of his own. He suggests that many a human need can only be
met by those who are prepared to "be present," and "by their
presence to provide a magnetic field of love into which others
would be attracted."

The heart of the matter is the attempt to be identified with the
other person by being in the profoundest sense of the word *available*. Most of us are never really available to other people. We are
too busy or too preoccupied. We are doing so much that others
either fear to interrupt or, if they do, never actually meet us because
it is only with half an ear that we attend to them.[86]

I venture to describe an instance of presence-evangelism with
which I once had personal contact. My home city of Washington is notorious, or was until very recently, for possessing
within its borders some of the worst slum districts in the land.
Two Christian laywomen, moved by Christian concern, though

under no missionary orders from their church headquarters, and with no resources beyond their modest salaries as employed secretaries, decided to launch out on a witnessing experiment. They moved into a vacant storefront apartment in the worst of our slum areas. Furnished simply, with, however, colorful cretonne curtains over freshly cleaned windows, the one-time store counter serving as a dining-room table, their home became a mission station by its mere presence in the midst of slum dirt and decay and human degradation. Of "silver and gold" they had little or none (one is reminded of the story in the third chapter of The Acts), but the mere fact that here was a ministry of caring in their midst, a ministry willing to recognize even the unclean as "brothers and sisters in Christ," and according the dignity of full human worth to "the least of these," had an incalculable effect on that slum neighborhood. I can confess to suffering many a sting of conscience when I returned from a visit to that storefront "colony of heaven" to my safe retreat on a cathedral close. Is there a substitute in the "imitation of Christ" for the first and primary form of incarnational evangelism, namely, that of presence? Yet how we shrink from such risking of ourselves in a ministry of real love of neighbors by becoming first of all precisely a "neighbor," in comparison with witnessing within a protected church environment! Hence the simplest listening ministry can frequently bring healing in its train. Loneliness is no longer singly borne. Someone cares. I have heard the gospel summarized in the two words, "God cares." One Christian, listening to a neighbor's tale of burdens, can, accordingly, be a sacrament of the divine love that was revealed on the cross.

I cannot resist giving one further illustration of nonverbal communication. If presence, service, and the simple act of listening can already be avenues of communication rich in rewards, an even more obviously nonverbal form of witness can be added to the list. This is "the look in the eye" with which we meet a fellowman. It is a fact easily verifiable that in most contacts with a friend, neighbor, or enemy, the eye comes into play before either tongue or ear. A look conveys acceptance or rejection though no word has yet been spoken.

A concrete instance of the importance of the look in the eye — important enough to involve the fate of entire nations — is a story told by a wise journalist-observer of our time. The author relates how he was present in Indonesia at the time when the Dutch colonial rule was about to end. In a conversation with the departing governor-general, the latter spoke bitter words: " I cannot understand it. Look what we have done for them. Look at the schools and the hospitals we have given them. We have done away with malaria, plague, and dysentery. Everyone has enough to eat. We have given them an honest and efficient administration and abolished war and piracy. Look at the roads, the railways, the industries — and yet they want us to go. Can you tell me why they want us to go? "

The author replied: " Yes, I think I can. I'm afraid it is because you've never had the right look in the eye when you spoke to them." And he adds the comment: " It may sound inadequate, but just think, for one moment, of the light that is in the eye of a human being when he looks at another human being he loves and respects as an equal. Then remember the look in the eye of the average European when he is in contact with ' a lesser breed without the law,' and you will understand what I mean. The difference between the two, I believe, is the explosive that has blown the Europeans out of one country after another during our time." [87]

These are only very partial visions of the opportunities for communicating the gospel that invite the scattered people of God to " the work of ministry." I have limited even these largely to nonverbal forms of witness, since it is in this area that the laity cannot delegate their ministry to the clerical order. The ministry of the Word can be a more specialized calling, though the laity, too, are, even in this area of witness, not relieved of responsibility. " Always be prepared," says I Peter 3:15, " to make a defense to any one who calls you to account for the hope that is in you, yet do it with gentleness and reverence."

Nonverbal witness may well have priority rights as preparation for the gospel, inasmuch as it may be the witness of life and action alone which will evoke questions addressed to the Christian about his faith. (How often we are tempted to rush in with answers to questions that have not been asked!) Eventually, however, the good news must be proclaimed. " How are men to call upon him in whom they have not believed? And how are they to believe in him of whom they have never heard? " (Rom. 10:14.) For this indispensable form of witness the opportunities for lay participation are, once again, almost limitless, though they cannot receive more than allusion here. Has not many a conversation at a dinner table, or even at a cocktail party, suddenly opened the locked gate of a neighbor's heart and revealed a hunger for the right spoken word? Most lay people would sadly confess that for this work of ministry — verbal now — they are ill-prepared. It is only as they have learned to be articulate about their faith in dialogue with fellow Christians that they can give an answer to those who ask.

There is no escape, indeed, from the strange paradox of the Christian life. The people of God are to be in the world and yet not of the world. The principalities and powers that tyrannize over our modern society are fearsome facts. We are all slaves of " conformity to this world " (cf. Rom. 12:2). We need merely turn the pages of popular books such as *The Organization Man* or *The Lonely Crowd* to see this tyranny of conformity vividly portrayed. The Christian, like his neighbor the religionless man, suffers under the rule of the prince of this world. But the Christian knows that such rule is temporary. Christ has already conquered the principalities and powers and the Christian can participate in that victory — in faith and hope.

We encounter a profound mystery here, yet one that is unveiled in Christian experience. There is such a thing as the freedom of the Christian man. The Christian can, by grace, live in the world yet be at the same time a citizen of heaven. Has this paradox of the Christian's freedom in the midst of apparent slavery ever received a more moving portrayal than in the seventh chapter of Paul's First Corinthians?

I mean, brethren, . . . let those who have wives live as though they had none, and those who mourn as though they were not mourning, and those who rejoice as though they were not rejoicing, and those who buy as though they had no goods, and those who deal with the world as though they had no dealings with it. For the form of this world is passing away. (Vs. 29-31.)

Can the laity of our churches acquire the power to live that kind of strange life of faith — to buy and sell "as though they had no goods," and to deal with the world "as though they had no dealings with it"? Impossible, we are tempted to say. And yet their membership in the body of Christ, which is both a gathered and a scattered people of God, is already a living symbol of this paradox. "The form of this world is passing away." Can those who know this set their heart on that which in the end will be but a "vanity of vanities"? The people of God, to fulfill their mission, must indeed become the scattered seed of the Kingdom. But the world in which they perform this mission is not their final home. They are "a colony of heaven." (Phil. 3:20, Moffatt's translation.) They are to live in the secular world, sharing in its workaday toil, its sorrows and its joys, yet as strangers and pilgrims: a costly life, and one which may involve mission under the cross. Allusion was made in an earlier chapter to the fact that God in Christ once became our neighbor and that neighborliness is to be our vocation also. But it was Christ's neighbors who brought him to the hill of Golgotha. "He came to his own home, and his own people received him not." (John 1:11.) Discipleship may mean crucifixion for those sharing in Christ's mission also — possibly to the end of time.

Dangers beset the scattered people of God if their acceptance of their mission lures them to mistake their mission habitat for their real home. Holy worldliness is one thing, as is a holy church. But mere worldliness is something else, as is a worldly church. The life of the people of God as scattered salt is not their final destiny. "As the Father has sent me, even so I send you" (John 20:21) — this is our Lord's commission to the disciple group. But those sent on mission are expected to return. The scattered people of God are to become the gathered people of God once more.

Perhaps the little text from the Sermon on the Mount — "You are the salt of the earth" — which can serve as a clue to an understanding of the mission call of the church, can itself give warning of the dangers encountered by that mission when it forgets its origin and its destiny. For that text has a sequel. Salt can lose its savor. "How," the Lord of the mission asks, "shall its saltness be restored? It is no longer good for anything except to be thrown out and trodden under foot by men." (Matt. 5:13.)

"Trodden under foot by men" — is there a more vivid picture possible for what has happened to thousands of Christian laymen and laywomen of our day and to even whole congregations? Scattered and lost, they have forgotten their way back to the Father's home.

The climactic promise of the gospel is one of a glorious gathering, and an invitation to those sent on mission to return rejoicing. "He that goes forth weeping, bearing the seed for sowing, shall come home with shouts of joy, bringing his sheaves with him." (Ps. 126:6.) The Shepherd calls into his sheepfold all his scattered sheep, even multitudes whom our mission has neglected, but whom he has found. A prophet of the older Covenant voices this vision of the end (Isa. 43:6-7):

> I will say to the north, Give up,
>   and to the south, Do not withhold;
> bring my sons from afar
>   and my daughters from the end of the earth,
> every one who is called by my name,
> whom I created for my glory,
> whom I formed and made.

Notes

1. Archibald M. Hunter, *The Message of the New Testament* (The Westminster Press, 1944), p. 122.

2. John Courtney Murray, an essay, " America's Four Conspiracies," in *Religion in America*, ed. by John Cogley (Meridian Books, Inc., 1958), p. 13.

3. G. Ernest Wright, *God Who Acts* (Alec R. Allenson, Inc., 1952), pp. 109 and 123.

4. Matthew Arnold, "To Marguerite" (*The Oxford Book of English Verse*, No. 749).

5. An analysis of this eminently useful distinction is found in Hendrik Kraemer's *The Communication of the Christian Faith*, pp. 11 f.

6. Interview with Arthur Godfrey, reported in *Time* (February 27, 1950), p. 75.

7. W. H. Auden, in an autobiographical essay in *Modern Canterbury Pilgrims* (Morehouse-Barlow Co., 1956), p. 35.

8. Klaus von Bismarck, "The Christian Vocabulary: An Obstacle to Communication?" in *The Ecumenical Review*, Vol. X (1957), pp. 6 f.

9. Karl Barth, *Church Dogmatics*, English translation (T. & T. Clark, Edinburgh, 1956), Vol. I, 2, pp. 297–325.

10. W. A. Visser 't Hooft, in *None Other Gods* (Harper & Row, Publishers, Inc., 1957), pp. 28 ff.

11. This is discussed at length in Martin E. Marty's *The New Shape of American Religion* (Harper & Row, Publishers, Inc., 1958).

12. Will Herberg, "Biblical Faith and Natural Religion" in *Theology Today* (January, 1955), p. 466.

13. Reinhold Niebuhr, "The Peril of Complacency in Our Nation" in *Christianity and Crisis* (February 8, 1954), p. 270.

14. David Head, *He Sent Leanness: A Book of Prayers for the Natural Man* (The Epworth Press, London, 1959), p. 19.

15. Abbé Georges Michonneau, *Revolution in a City Parish*, pp. 20 f.

16. A full analysis can be found in H. Richard Niebuhr's *Christ and Culture* (Harper & Row, Publishers, Inc., 1951).

17. An evaluation of this new monasticism and of what it may mean for the renewal of the church is an article entitled "Worldly Holiness" in the British journal *Frontier* (January, 1958). See also a World Council of Churches' pamphlet, *Signs of Renewal*.

18. Cited from an essay in a World Student Christian Federation pamphlet *The Life and Mission of the Church* (1957), p. 14.

19. Hans Pohlmann, *Die Metanoia als Zeitbegriff der amtlichen Frömmigkeit* (Leipzig, 1938), p. 19.

20. John Oman, *Grace and Personality* (Cambridge University Press, London, 1919), pp. 75 f.

21. George MacLeod, *Only One Way Left* (Iona Community, Glasgow, 1956), p. 38.

22. See also Kraemer, *op. cit.*, pp. 111–113.

23. *Die mündige Welt*, two volumes (Kaiser Verlag, München, 1955 and 1956).

24. Dietrich Bonhoeffer, *Prisoner for God: Letters and Papers from Prison*, tr. by R. H. Fuller (The Macmillan Company, 1954), p. 124. Quotations used by permission.

25. *Ibid.*, p. 124.

26. *Ibid.*, p. 122.

27. Dietrich Bonhoeffer, *The Cost of Discipleship*, tr. by R. H. Fuller (S.C.M. Press, Ltd., London, 1948); *Sanctorum Communio* (Kaiser Verlag, München, 1954); *Life Together*, tr. by J. W. Doberstein (Harper & Row, Publishers, Inc., 1954). Quotations from *Life Together* are used by permission.

28. Sören Kierkegaard, *Either-Or*, tr. by Walter Lowrie (Princeton University Press, 1944), Vol. II, p. 135.

29. Horst Symanowski, *Gegen die Weltfremdheit* (Kaiser Verlag, München, 1960), p. 19.

30. Gustaf Wingren, *The Living Word* (S.C.M. Press, Ltd., London, 1960), p. 142.

31. Karl Barth, *Church Dogmatics* (Vol. I, 2, pp. 444 ff.) also

contains a rewarding — and disturbing — presentation of what "neighbor" should mean to us.

32. Symanowski, *op. cit.*, p. 19.

33. Gibson Winter, *The Suburban Captivity of the Churches* (Doubleday & Co., Inc., 1961), p. 72.

34. *The Collected Poems of Thomas Hardy* (The Macmillan Company, 1940), p. 306. Used by permission.

35. Ida Friederike Coudenhove, *The Nature of Sanctity* (Sheed & Ward, Inc., 1933), pp. 96 f.

36. Jean-Paul Sartre, quoted in an article by A. J. Guérard, "French and American Pessimism" in *Harper's Magazine* (September, 1945), p. 270.

37. A contemporary validation of the fact that fear of "other people" haunts our common life is the following comment of an observer of the race relations problem in the American South: "I do not think that Southerners are afraid of the pope or the Communists or the Negroes; they are afraid of each other. They are afraid of 'what people will say,' of 'getting out of line,' of appearing 'different.'" In an article by C. Van Woodward, "The New South," in *The Washington Post* (July 9, 1961).

38. These paragraphs owe much to an essay by William H. Poteat, "On the Meaning of Grace," in *The Hibbert Journal* (January, 1959), pp. 156–160.

39. Blaise Pascal, *Pensées*, tr. by W. F. Trotter (Modern Library, Inc., 1941), p. 41.

40. Jean-Paul Sartre, *Being and Nothingness*, tr. by Hazel E. Barnes (Philosophical Library, Inc., 1956), p. 255.

41. T. S. Eliot, *The Cocktail Party* (Harcourt, Brace and World, Inc., 1950), p. 134. Used by permission.

42. Karl Heim, *Christian Faith and Natural Science* (Harper & Row, Publishers, Inc., 1953), pp. 124 f.

43. Alec Vidler, *Christ's Strange Work* (Longmans, Green & Co., Ltd., London, 1944), p. 40. It should be emphasized, of course — and Vidler's book clarifies this issue also — that the Sermon is not only fulfillment of the law, but prophecy of life under grace in the Kingdom as well. The title of Vidler's book suggests that Christ's "strange work" as interpreter of the demands of God is preparation for his "work" as Redeemer. Another book, *The Meaning of Christ*, by Robert Clyde Johnson (The Westminster Press, 1958), also contains an excellent corrective to the humanist under-

standing of the Christ of the New Testament in language meant for the layman. Any church school teacher could profit from his portrayal of Jesus as " Accuser " (pp. 22–26).

44. Dietrich Bonhoeffer, *Life Together,* pp. 90 f.

45. Used by permission of Joseph W. O'Brien, Episcopal student chaplain at Duke University.

46. This analogical clue to an existential understanding of " justification " has received masterful exposition in one of Rudolf Bultmann's essays, " Grace and Freedom " in *Essays Philosophical and Theological* (S.C.M. Press, Ltd., London, 1955), pp. 168–181.

47. M. A. C. Warren, *The Christian Mission* (S.C.M. Press, Ltd., London, 1951), p. 5.

48. One of the major actions of the Assembly of the World Council of Churches in New Delhi (1961) was the " marriage " of the two Councils. The International Missionary Council became a division within the World Council of Churches' own structure, its new title being the Division of World Mission and Evangelism. Bishop Lesslie Newbigin, until the merger the Executive Secretary of the International Missionary Council, became the executive secretary of the new division.

49. Lesslie Newbigin, *One Body, One Gospel, One World* (International Missionary Council pamphlet, 1961), p. 26.

50. The title of an important issue of the *Federation News* (No. 5, 1957).

51. Winter, *op. cit.,* pp. 37 and 84 ff.

52. " Evangelism — the Mission of the Church to Those Outside Her Life " in *The Ecumenical Review* (October, 1953).

53. G. Paul Musselman, *The Church on the Urban Frontier,* p. 50.

54. *Ibid.,* p. 33.

55. Emil Brunner, *The Misunderstanding of the Church* (The Westminster Press, 1955), p. 14.

56. J. C. Hoekendijk, " The Church in Missionary Thinking " in *The International Review of Missions* (July, 1952), pp. 332 and 336. The debate on the emergence of " church-centered evangelism " in recent ecumenical discourse is partly summarized in Wilhelm Anderson, *Towards a Theology of Missions* (S.C.M. Press, Ltd., London, 1955). A wise corrective to Hoekendijk's extreme views can be found in Lesslie Newbigin, *The Household of God,* pp. 168–170.

57. Brunner, *op. cit.*, pp. 48 f.

58. Paul Tillich, *Systematic Theology* (University of Chicago Press, 1951), Vol. I, pp. 176 f.

59. My excursus on group dynamics consists largely of an edited version of an article of my own " Group Dynamics and the Church " in *Theology Today* (January, 1954), pp. 511–524.

60. Adolf Harnack, *The Expansion of Christianity in the First Three Centuries*, tr. by James Moffatt (G. P. Putnam's Sons, 1905), Vol. II, p. 50.

61. John Wesley, cited in Colin W. Williams, *John Wesley's Theology Today* (Abingdon Press, 1960), p. 151.

62. From the encyclical *Vehementer* of Pius X (1906), cited in J. S. Whale, *Christian Doctrine* (Cambridge University Press, London, 1942), pp. 13 f. It is only fair to add here, however, that many voices in Roman Catholicism today speak correctively of such extreme views. Some of these will receive attention later in this chapter.

63. *Doctrine in the Church of England:* The Report of the Commission on Christian Doctrine Appointed by the Archbishops of Canterbury and York in 1922. (Macmillan & Co., Ltd., London, 1938), pp. 114 f. and 157.

64. Robert S. Michaelson, " The Protestant Ministry in America," in *The Ministry in Historical Perspective*, ed. by H. Richard Niebuhr and Daniel D. Williams (Harper & Row, Publishers, Inc., 1956), p. 284.

65. Yves M. J. Congar, O.P., *Lay People in the Church: A Study for a Theology of the Laity*, tr. by Donald Attwater, p. 45.

66. Hendrik Kraemer, *A Theology of the Laity* (The Westminster Press, 1958).

67. *Evanston Assembly Report* (World Council of Churches, 1954), Section VI, p. 11.

68. Bonhoeffer, *Life Together*, pp. 17–19.

69. Kraemer, *A Theology of the Laity*, p. 72.

70. Barth, *Church Dogmatics*, Vol. I, 2, p. 453.

71. Congar, *op. cit.*, p. 160.

72. Didascalia, chapter 13. Quoted by W. J. Pythian-Adams in *Church Quarterly Review*, June, 1943, p. 28. The writer of the epistle to the Hebrews (ch. 10:24-25) found it necessary to issue a similar appeal to the Christians of even New Testament times.

73. Congar, *op. cit.*, p. 51.

74. It ought to be taken for granted that a plea for giving back to the laity the gift of dialogue in a Christian fellowship does not imply artificial revival of some of the bizarre forms of " speaking with tongues " which arose in the Corinthian church. Paul does not encourage such license either. There is surely need, however, of recovering what the New Testament does encourage, namely, "prophecy," though what this means calls for wise exegesis. Alec Vidler suggests that here is a topic to which Biblical theologians could well direct further attention. See his *Christian Belief and This World*, the chapter entitled " Are We Also Among the Prophets? " (The Seabury Press, Inc., 1957), pp. 55–84.

75. Margaret Frakes, *Bridges to Understanding* (Muhlenberg Press, 1960).

76. Ernest W. Southcott, *The Parish Comes Alive* (Morehouse-Gorham Co., Inc., 1956).

77. Smith, *op. cit.*, p. 81.

78. W. A. Visser 't Hooft, ed., *New Delhi Speaks* (Association Press, 1962), pp. 49, 50.

79. Harry A. DeWire, *The Christian as Communicator*, p. 49. This basic fact of human, communal existence is given full exposition on pp. 45 ff. The book is an invaluable guide for personal evangelism.

80. Karl Barth, *Church Dogmatics*, Vol. I, 2, p. 449.

81. DeWire, *op. cit.*, p. 71.

82. R. Voillaume, *Seeds of the Desert: The Legacy of Charles de Foucauld* (Fides Publishers' Association, London, 1955), pp. 17 and 19.

83. Both quotations appear in Rene Bazin's *Charles de Foucauld, Hermit and Explorer*, tr. by Peter Keelan (Burns, Oates & Washbourne, Ltd., London, 1923), p. 307.

84. The story of one such mission is told in E. R. Wickham's *Church and People in an Industrial City* (Lutterworth Press, London, 1957).

85. Florence Allshorn, cited in Max Warren's *Challenge and Response* (Morehouse-Barlow Co., 1959), p. 75.

86. Warren, *op. cit.*, p. 75.

87. Laurens Van Der Post, *The Dark Eye in Africa* (William Morrow & Co., Inc., 1954), pp. 116 f.

Annotated Bibliography

This bibliography — of necessity selective — omits many titles of books or articles cited in the text of the lectures. Publication information on these will be found in the notes appended to the chapters in which the citations occur.

Bachman, John W., *The Church in the World of Radio-Television.* Association Press, 1960.
This book supplements, on the level of practical applications, such more theological evaluations of mass communication media as those by Martin Marty and Roland Mushat Frye (see below).

Bonhoeffer, Dietrich, *Prisoner for God: Letters and Papers from Prison,* tr. by R. H. Fuller (The Macmillan Company, 1954); and *Life Together,* tr. by J. W. Doberstein (Harper & Row, Publishers, Inc., 1954).
The several books by Bonhoeffer which are cited and discussed in these lectures, particularly in Chapter I, need no further introduction in this bibliography. Those who desire a general introduction to Bonhoeffer's life and thought are referred to *The Theology of Dietrich Bonhoeffer,* by John D. Godsey (The Westminster Press, 1960).

Boyd, Malcolm, *Crisis in Communication.* Doubleday & Co., Inc., 1957.
Written in a lively style by a one-time publicity director in the motion picture industry, but now a minister in the Protestant Episcopal Church, this book introduces the reader to the challenge which the churches encounter in their inevitable rivalry with the mass communication media of our time. It pleads for an honest dialogue between the church and the world as the latter is portrayed in secular art and storytelling.

131

Brown, Roger, *Words and Things*. The Free Press of Glencoe, 1958.

For those willing to explore, even only under secular guidance, the mysteries of language, this book could be a companion volume to the one by S. I. Hayakawa (see below).

Cartwright, D., and Zander, A., *Group Dynamics: Research and Theory*. Harper & Row, Publishers, Inc., 1956.

An advanced textbook in the field of sociometric research — a collection of essay contributions by a score of competent authors.

Casteel, John L., *Spiritual Renewal Through Personal Groups*. Association Press, 1957.

The " cell movement " and similar agencies for communication by way of group experience have received a good deal of attention in this book. Dr. Casteel's survey of such entrance into Christian faith and life is an invaluable contribution to the widespread rediscovery of this form of evangelism going on throughout the Christian world.

Cleland, James T., *The True and Lively Word* (Kellogg Lectures at the Episcopal Theological School for 1953). Charles Scribner's Sons, 1954.

The word " lively " in the title applies to the style of this book as well as to its contents. Although dealing mainly with the task of the modern preacher — the author being a noted professor of homiletics — the book is well worth the attention of any layman who would like to see what sermon literature can be like when a master of communication shares his insights.

Congar, Yves M. J., *Lay People in the Church: A Study for a Theology of the Laity,* tr. by Donald Attwater. The Newman Press, 1957.

This is the most thorough study yet available of the ministry of the laity in Christian tradition. The author is a Roman Catholic; hence, for a balanced view, the student should give equal attention to Hendrik Kraemer's *A Theology of the Laity* (see below), a more modest, but no less provocative, treatment of the ministry of the laity by a Protestant theologian.

DeWire, Harry A., *The Christian as Communicator* (Westminster Studies in Christian Communication, ed. by Kendig Brubaker Cully). The Westminster Press, 1961.

Most books dealing with the problem of communication center attention on the church's corporate responsibility and that of its office-bearers. Here, however, is an exploration of how even the single Christian layman can become an effective evangelist. Few volumes devoted to Christian communication can so readily solicit the attention of the church's laity — a laity being awakened in our day to their privilege as the church's front-line witnessing army.

Dillistone, F. W., *Christianity and Communication*. William Collins Sons & Co., Ltd., London, 1956.
A study, largely historical, but also one cognizant of our contemporary situation, of the always changing task of the churches to win a hearing for the gospel. A competent and stimulating survey by a Church of England theologian.

Douty, Mary Alice, *How to Work with Church Groups*. Abingdon Press, 1960.
Designed for the guidance of leaders of groups in a local church. Simple and practical.

Ferré, Frederick, *Language, Logic and God*. Harper & Row, Publishers, Inc., 1960.
A readable introduction to contemporary linguistic philosophy as it bears on theological discourse. Though this philosophic discipline has received little or no mention in my book, it deserves attention. It will play an increasing role in theological literature in coming years.

Frye, Roland Mushat, *Perspective on Man: Literature and the Christian Tradition*. The Westminster Press, 1961.
A teacher of English literature introduces theologians and readers generally to the almost limitless treasures of insight into religious truth to be found in our literary heritage. His survey ranges widely over the centuries from Greek tragedy to T. S. Eliot. He finds the English poet Milton especially relevant for throwing light on theological problems which still concern our age.

Hayakawa, S. I., *Language in Thought and Action*. Harcourt, Brace and World, Inc., 1949.
This book is something of a classic. Though not dealing with Christian communication as such, it is an introduction to the general subject of semantics — one that is relevant to all forms of language communication.

Kelley, Alden D., *Christianity and Political Responsibility* (Westminster Studies in Christian Communication, ed. by Kendig Brubaker Cully). The Westminster Press, 1961.
" Communication will take place through incarnation, participa-

tion in the human enterprise, not by exhortation from the sanctuary." The book is an enlargement on this key sentence. The author pleads for an incarnational theology as guide for the church's dialogue with the world.

Knowles, Malcolm and Hulda, *Introduction to Group Dynamics.* Association Press, 1959.
A very simple introduction to this new field of research. Though secular in anchorage, the book is good for use with lay people in the churches which are exposing themselves to group experience.

Kraemer, Hendrik, *The Communication of the Christian Faith.* The Westminster Press, 1956.
Probably the most comprehensive book on the subject yet written in English. Dr. Kraemer, layman missionary, theologian of the first rank, ecumenical statesman (he was Director of the Ecumenical Institute of the World Council of Churches in Geneva during the first five years of its life), is equipped for giving us a survey of the ministry of communication in Christian history as no other scholar of our day. The reader will be especially impressed by the profound insight of the author into the Biblical imperative for the witnessing vocation.

Kraemer, Hendrik, *A Theology of the Laity.* The Westminster Press, 1958.
A pioneering study of the opportunities for evangelism latent in a revival in the churches of the ministry of the laity. The author (see also the note on the previous volume) was, during the preparatory years for the Evanston Assembly of the World Council of Churches, Chairman of the Council's Department on the Laity. No more competent study on the role of the laity in the church by a Protestant author has as yet appeared.

Luccock, Halford E., *Communicating the Gospel.* Harper & Row, Publishers, Inc., 1954.
A voluminous author, helpful through his writings to a whole generation of preachers, summarizes here in brief compass some of his long matured insights.

MacLeod, George, *Only One Way Left.* Iona Community, Glasgow, 1956.
This is only one of several books and pamphlets emerging from the Iona Community in Scotland — an experiment in the revival of Christian "life in community." Important for an insight into one of the most promising church renewal movements of our time.

Marty, Martin, *The Improper Opinion* (Westminster Studies in Christian Communication, ed. by Kendig Brubaker Cully). The Westminster Press, 1961.

The author's earlier book, *The New Shape of American Religion*, has introduced him to a wide reading public. This volume is narrower in scope, but it deals with a communication problem no less contemporary. Mass media of communication are here to stay for the foreseeable future. Their handicaps for Christian communication are realistically presented by Dr. Marty, but also equally realistic guidance for their use as servants of the gospel.

Michonneau, Abbé Georges, *Revolution in a City Parish*. The Newman Press, 1951.

A penetrating appraisal by a Roman Catholic parish priest in Paris of the gulf that exists today between the church and its secular environment.

Mollegen, Albert T., *Christianity and Modern Man*. The Bobbs-Merrill Company, Inc., 1961.

A seminary teacher with a long experience in conducting discussion forums for lay people here sets down in writing a kind of " apology " for Christianity. One of the best introductions to the Christian faith designed for the modern educated man available today.

Moreau, Jules Laurence, *Language and Religious Language* (Westminster Studies in Christian Communication, ed. by Kendig Brubaker Cully). The Westminster Press, 1961.

A volume introducing the reader to the rich harvest of insights that linguistic research is placing at our disposal. Somewhat technical early chapters are followed by essays of immediate value for ministers and church teachers.

Musselman, G. Paul, *The Church on the Urban Frontier*. The Seabury Press, Inc., 1960.

This is a lively presentation of the newest home mission field on the American scene — the inner city. The author, for some years Executive Secretary for Evangelism of the National Council of the Churches of Christ in the U.S.A., shares with church leaders his personal experience as a pioneer investigator of our urban mission frontier.

Newbigin, Lesslie, *The Household of God*. Friendship Press, 1954.

This book has attained the reputation of a modern classic. For an understanding of a doctrine of the church as " mission," no better guide has yet appeared. Although the insights of the book are theologically profound, it is written in a style that can appeal to laymen as well as to ministers.

Philips, Gerard, *The Role of the Laity in the Church*. Fides Publishers Association, Chicago, 1956.
A companion study to that by Congar (see above) of the apostolate of the laity, as this is emerging into prominence in the Roman Catholic Church. Some would say that, while Congar's earlier volume is superior on the historical side, this book wins in the comparison by way of offering guidance for the church's future strategy.

Read, David H. C., *The Communication of the Gospel*. S.C.M. Press, Ltd., London, 1952.
A pioneer volume in its field. The author, originally from Scotland, but now for some years pastor of a large New York congregation, shares with his brother ministers his convictions concerning their vocation as communicators of the gospel. Lively and practical.

Sellers, James E., *The Outsider and the Word of God*. Abingdon Press, 1961.
The author traces the ministry of communication from the church's earliest days to our time and discusses with much theological wisdom the call to the churches to meet contemporary needs. His particular interest, in the second half of the book, centers on the problems encountered by the religious journalist and by those responsible for religious television and radio.

Smith, R. Gregor, *The New Man*. Harper & Row, Publishers, Inc., 1956.
This book is an expanded comment on the view of " man come of age " which Dietrich Bonhoeffer has introduced into the theological discourse of our time. A provocative volume.

Tillich, Paul, *Theology of Culture*. Oxford University Press, 1954.
Although all the chapters in this book are relevant to the topic of communication, of most value to students in this area of concern will be the concluding essay with the actual title, " Communicating the Christian Message: A Question to Christian Ministers and Teachers." Dr. Tillich is himself a master of the art of bridging the gulf between the Christian faith and our secular culture. His insights into our common task, accordingly, can prove invaluable.

Warren, Max, *The Christian Imperative*. Charles Scribner's Sons, 1955.

A moving presentation of the mission call to the churches. Companion volumes by the same author, one of the most trusted missionary statesmen of our time, are: *The Christian Mission* (S.C.M. Press, Ltd., London, 1951) and *Challenge and Response* (Morehouse-Barlow Co., 1959).

Weber, H. R., *The Communication of the Gospel to Illiterates* (International Missionary Council Research Pamphlet Number 4). S.C.M. Press, Ltd., London, 1956.

Although this is a booklet, it deserves full attention since it is one of few explorations of a communicating ministry that the churches might well exercise at home as well as in primitive social environments. We have religious illiterates with us also. The reader will discover to his surprise that the story of the Bible can be told by way of simple diagrams and pictorial symbols — a method of communication that could be of help in many church school classrooms.

Winter, Gibson, *The Suburban Captivity of the Churches.* Doubleday & Co., Inc., 1961.

A provocative sociological analysis of the "organization church" (the author's phrase) which has become the norm in America. Often disturbing criticism, however, is balanced by helpful suggestions for the renewal of the churches as they submit themselves to the call to mission, especially in the inner city which suburbia has left behind.

Index

Date Due
